STEAM TRACTION ON THE ROAD

STEAM TRACTION ON THE ROAD

From Trevithick to Stanley

Anthony Burton

PEN & SWORD
TRANSPORT

AN IMPRINT OF PEN & SWORD BOOKS LTD.
YORKSHIRE - PHILADELPHIA

First published in Great Britain in 2018 by
PEN & SWORD TRANSPORT
An imprint of
Pen & Sword Books Ltd
Yorkshire - Philadelphia

ISBN 978 1 52670 151 0

Typeset in 10.5/13.5 pt Palatino
Typeset by Aura Technology and Software Services, India
Printed and bound in India by Replika Pvt. Ltd.

Pen & Sword Books Ltd incorporates the Imprints of Pen & Sword Books Archaeology, Atlas, Aviation, Battleground, Discovery, Family History, History, Maritime, Military, Naval, Politics, Railways, Select, Transport, True Crime, Fiction, Frontline Books, Leo Cooper, Praetorian Press, Seaforth Publishing, Wharncliffe and White Owl.

For a complete list of Pen & Sword titles please contact

PEN & SWORD BOOKS LIMITED
47 Church Street, Barnsley, South Yorkshire, S70 2AS, England
E-mail: enquiries@pen-and-sword.co.uk
Website: www.pen-and-sword.co.uk

Or
PEN AND SWORD BOOKS
1950 Lawrence Rd, Havertown, PA 19083, USA
E-mail: Uspen-and-sword@casematepublishers.com
Website: www.penandswordbooks.com

Contents

Introduction

When anyone thinks about the development of steam power in the world of transport, the first thing likely to come into the mind is the steam railway. This is perfectly understandable, for it had an immense impact on life in countries all round the world. Yet steam vehicles appeared on the road before they took to the tracks. It has to be admitted that the road vehicles did not have quite as dramatic an effect in changing society as did the railways, but they did bring great changes to many aspects of life, not least in agriculture. The potential was there for greater development but time and again the attempts to develop an efficient steam transport system for the roads was hampered not by technology, but by a series of often absurdly over-cautious restrictions imposed by government. In this book, we shall be looking at all these different manifestations of steam on the road. But why should anyone be interested in a form of transport that had a limited effect and was more or less redundant nearly a century ago? There are several possible answers, but for many of us it is simply a matter of a fascination with these magnificent machines.

I am writing these words on that modern technological miracle, a computer. But if I were to dismantle it, there would be nothing in the components that would help in understanding how it works. We can read about how the computer works, even learn how to programme it for ourselves, but the physical machine gives nothing away. The same is true of many modern machines we take for granted. But if we look at a steam engine, even the most complicated version, it is still possible to work out exactly what does what and how. It may take a bit of time, but even without specialist engineering knowledge, the general principles are easily understood, from even a quick inspection. Here is a fire that heats water to make steam, and that steam will try to expand. If we allow it into a cylinder with a piston, it will push that piston along until the vapour can escape the cylinder. And if it cannot escape, the cylinder will burst; the power of steam should not be underrated. Add mechanical connections to the piston, and its backward and forward movement can turn a wheel – and if you can turn a wheel you can make something move. Of course, the machines themselves are far more complex than this short description might suggest, but the idea is simple. And we can actually see it happening.

The steam engine is elemental, and somehow has a very human feel to it. We have to feed the fire that makes the steam ourselves if we want to make a traction engine work. And when it moves, we can watch the fascinating interplay of the different linkages. It is immensely satisfying and, of course, for those lucky enough to have a chance to work with these machines it is even more of an exhilarating experience. I shall always remember my first trip out on a traction engine, when I was entrusted with the steering and that great lover of all things steam, Teddy Boston, was driving. We charged around the narrow country lanes near his vicarage in Leicestershire and what surprised me most was how what appeared to be a cumbersome beast responded so readily to the controls. It brought home to me that this was in fact a very sophisticated and beautifully engineered machine. I had been involved with steam in other forms over the years, particularly stationary steam engines, but this provoked my interest in road vehicles and their history, hence this book. Over the next few pages we shall be looking at the development of steam road power over a period of over a century and celebrating the ingenuity of the engineers, some well-known, others anonymous, who gave us the great variety of these road vehicles, many of which still steam for our pleasure and delight.

CHAPTER ONE

Beginnings

Almost a century had passed since the invention of the first successful steam engine before engines went on the move. The story of steam began with the need for more efficient pumps to drain water from deep mines. There was an early device, known as 'The Miner's Friend' designed by Captain Savery in 1698, but it did not lead to any further developments and was never widely used. At the beginning of the eighteenth century, however, a Dartmouth man, Thomas Newcomen, began experimenting with a different idea and the first of his engines was installed at a coal mine at Dudley in the Black Country in 1812. Pumps were worked by means of an up and down motion of the pump rods – in its simplest form by working the handle at the village pump. Newcomen's pumps were on an altogether grander scale. The pump rods were hung from one end of a pivoted overhead beam, and dropped down under their own weight. What Newcomen supplied was a force to raise them up again. At the opposite end of the beam was a piston fitting snugly into a cylinder. Steam was allowed in under the piston and then condensed by spraying with cold water. This created a partial vacuum under the piston and air pressure forced it down, pulling down that end of the beam and so lifting the rods at the other end. Pressure equalised, gravity took over again to pull the rods down, and set in motion the see-sawing of the beam and the rise and fall of the pump rods.

Newcomen's engine undoubtedly did the job it was designed to do, and soon the massive engines were nodding over shafts from the tin and copper mines of Cornwall to coal mines in Scotland. The engine was, however, extremely inefficient, thanks to the energy needed for constantly having to reheat the cylinder after each stroke. This was not particularly important at coal mines where fuel that might not have been good enough for sale was quite adequate for feeding the boilers. It was far more troublesome in Cornwall, where fuel was mainly imported across the water from South Wales at a great cost. The Cornish engineers did their best to try to improve the engine, but gains were only marginal. It was a young Scottish instrument maker at Glasgow University who spotted the nature of the problem and saw a solution.

Thomas Newcomen installed this, his first atmospheric engine, at a colliery in Dudley. For almost all of the next two hundred years the only steam engines in use in Britain were immense beam engines, such as this. All these engines worked at low pressure and the massive stone-built engine house was an essential part of the structure.

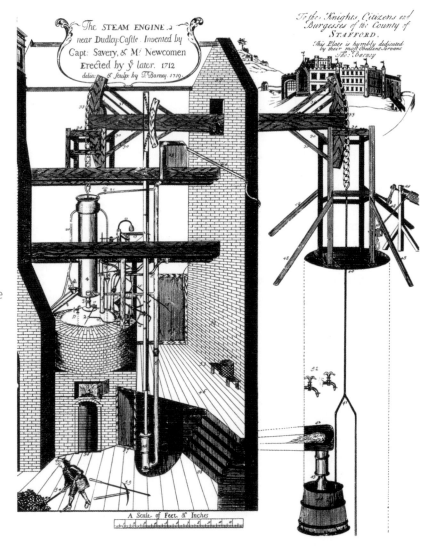

James Watt's solution was to condense the steam in a separate vessel so that the cylinder would not lose heat by being constantly drenched in cold water. But heat would still escape through the open top of the cylinder. To solve this problem, he closed the top and instead of air pressure pushing down the piston, he used steam pressure. The atmospheric engine had become a true steam engine. Watt went into partnership with the Birmingham businessman Matthew Boulton and set up a company to manufacture the new engines, and they took out a patent to protect the invention. It soon became clear, that by allowing the steam to be forced alternately onto either side of the piston, there was no need for pump rods to provide the movement in one direction. And if the piston could be moved up and down using steam alone, it would be a simple matter to convert this up and down motion to turn a wheel. The first application was to drive the machinery of textile mills, but others saw new possibilities.

Given that all the early development of steam power had taken place in Britain, it is perhaps a little surprising that the first successful experiments to use steam engines for land transport took place in France. Perhaps British inventors were put off by Watt's all-embracing patent. It was a retired French army officer, Nicolas Joseph Cugnot, who had seen the problems involved in lugging heavy artillery around using horses, and decided that a steam engine might offer a better solution. He set about designing a steam tractor and his prototype, a quite extraordinary device, was put through its paces in 1769. It was a three-wheeled vehicle. The spherical boiler was suspended above the single front wheel and steam fed down to pistons on either side of the same wheel. These connected with a ratchet to provide the drive. As that same

Nicholas Joseph Cugnot's was the world's first ever steam-powered road vehicle. The prototype first appeared in 1769 and was intended to be used as a tractor for artillery. It was never accepted by the military and after its unsuccessful trial this model, the second version of 1770, eventually found a home in the Musée des Arts et Métiers in Paris.

wheel was also the one that could be steered it must have been all but unmanageable. He built a second version in 1770, which was no more manageable than the first. In fact a story, probably apocryphal, has it that on the first run it got out of control and demolished a brick wall at the French arsenal, at which point the authorities banned it. Whether true or not, what we do know is that the experiment was never followed up. The prototype was, in any case, virtually useless in battle conditions as it lacked an essential ingredient – a feed pump. As a result, when the boiler ran low on water the whole machine had to be stopped, everything allowed to cool down and then refilled. Meanwhile, presumably, the 'old fashioned' horse-drawn carriage would have hurried on to the front.

France was to see a far more successful experiment with steam when the Marquis Jouffroy d'Abbans devised a paddle steamer that was sufficiently successful for it to go into service on the River Saône in 1783. Any chances that France might become a centre for steam innovation vanished, however, when the country was plunged into political revolution. The technological events in France went largely unnoticed across the Channel in Britain. Steamboat development did get under way before the end of the eighteenth century, but work on road vehicles took a little longer.

James Watt's patent stifled competition and there was one point on which he was adamant: high-pressure steam was anathema. If you needed more power, you simply built larger engines and pumping engines became enormous; the largest ever built by the Cornish firm of Harvey of Hayle had a massive 144-inch diameter cylinder. These monsters were firmly and immovably rooted to the spot. Among the places where Boulton & Watt received a huge welcome at first was Cornwall, but the Cornish engineers were used to making their own innovations and changes. This was firmly resisted by Boulton & Watt and those who tried to introduce changes soon found themselves on the wrong end of lawsuits. One of the men who was opposed to police affairs in Cornwall, supervising the erection and use of engines and tracking down steam pirates trying to evade the patent was William Murdoch (sometimes spelt Murdock). Yet he was the man who was secretly working on the heretical notion of using high-pressure steam to create a powered road vehicle.

Murdoch produced a working model, which, like Cugnot's was three-wheeled, but rather more manageable. The boiler was set at one end of a platform, with a vertical cylinder embedded in it.

William Murdoch was the first to attempt to design a steam carriage in Britain. He never progressed further than constructing and experimenting with a model. He was about to apply for a patent in 1795, but his employers, Boulton & Watt, who were violently opposed to the whole idea, made it clear that if he did so he would have to look for a new job. He abandoned the experiment and his model is now in the Birmingham Museum and Art Gallery. A full scale version based on the model has now been built by the Murdoch Flyer Project.

A beam took the drive from the piston rod to a crank to turn the front wheel. In order to keep his activities secret, he made his trials at night. On one of these nights, he set the model in motion in a narrow lane by the church in Redruth. He set off to trot after it, when he heard anguished cries. It turned out that the local vicar had also been coming home in the dark, when he saw a fiery monster approaching. He was, he later declared, certain he had met 'the Evil One'. The vicar was calmed down, but inevitably news of the experiment reached the ears of Boulton & Watt. Murdoch had broken all their most cherished rules; the engine did not use a condenser at all, but worked with what was then referred to as 'strong steam'. By 1795 he had built three

The Cornish engineer Richard Trevithick began experimenting with high pressure steam and, like Murdoch, first tried out his ideas for a portable form of steam power and for steam transport by building models. This was his third model of 1797 and is now in the Steam Museum at Strafes, Ireland.

experimental models and was ready to apply for a patent. He set off for London on the pretext of looking for skilled men to come to Cornwall, but was confronted by Matthew Boulton, who made it clear that the company was aware what was going in and would vigorously oppose his application. The heretic was given a straight choice – continue his experiments and leave the company or remain in an important and well paid job. He wisely chose the latter and was to go on to make other discoveries and inventions, notably introducing gas lighting

One other early designer was Robert Fourness of Otley, who built a curious model steam carriage in 1788. It was a three-wheeled vehicle and had three inverted cylinders that drove a crankshaft. This was connected to the axle by spur gearing, but only one of the driving wheels was keyed to the main axle in order to make it easier to get round sharp bends. The exhaust steam was passed into a tank to preheat the feedwater for the boiler and water could be supplied by a feed pump, worked by a crosshead from one of the piston rods. There is no evidence that it ever reached beyond the model stage, although as Fourness was a successful engineer with his own works, first in Sheffield then in Gainsborough, there would have been nothing to prevent him constructing working machines. However, we have no information on the fate of the prototype and Fourness himself died at an early age. It was to be more than a decade before an actual full-scale engine would be built. It was left to one of the pirates who had plagued Boulton & Watt for many years to take developments much further.

Richard Trevithick was born into a Cornish mining family, and his father was one of a number of engineers who had developed improvements to the old Newcomen engines – and the son saw no reason why he should not do the same to a Boulton & Watt. The fact that this was strictly forbidden did not prevent his trying and, inevitably, he found himself served with an injunction, prohibiting further attempts at piracy of the patent. But the law could not stop him thinking about the problem. The main feature of the Boulton & Watt engine was the separate condenser, but Trevithick wondered what would happen if, instead of condensing the exhaust steam, you simply let it blow away into the atmosphere. He consulted a scientific friend, Davies Gilbert, and asked him how much pressure would be lost if he raised steam pressure to several atmospheres and did not use the condenser. The answer was simple: one atmosphere. Atmospheric pressure at sea level is roughly 15 pounds per square inch (psi). Gilbert reported that 'he never saw a man more delighted'. Trevithick decided that he could use high pressure steam to produce a new kind of whim engine – the machine used to wind men and materials up and down the shaft. His workshop was his kitchen table and he set about building a model, which was given a ceremonial trial. The honour of stoking the 'strong iron kettle' went to Davies Gilbert, and the honour of opening the steam cock went

In 1801 Trevithick built his first full-sized road locomotive, which ran with great success at Camborne, Cornwall on Christmas Eve of that year. In the New Year, he and a friend set out for Tehidy House to show the engine off to Lord and Lady de Dunstanville. They never arrived, having turned over in a ditch, where the engine was abandoned and later caught fire. This working replica, built by the Trevithick Society to celebrate the bicentenary, did however make it and the photograph shows it outside Tehidy House.

to Lady de Dunstanville, of a prominent mine owning family. The experiment was a success, and Trevithick set about designing a boiler that could safely produce steam at 50psi, more than enough to compensate for the loss of one atmosphere. Earlier boilers had been little better than oversized kettles, but this was a new type, in which the heat was supplied by hot gases from the firebox passing through the water in a tube attached to the chimney. He improved the system, doubling the area in contact with the water, by bending the tube into a U-shape. Davies Gilbert, having provided him with the information on atmospheric pressure, now came to inspect the new boiler:

> 'The boiler was of Cast Iron and its upper surface flat, the Fuel being applied within the Boiler in wrought iron Tubes. We stood near the boiler, i.e. not upon it. When I came deliberately to calculate the Pressure exerted on the Flat surface of Iron, I drew the conclusion that perhaps I had never been in such imminent danger.'

In spite of Gilbert's qualms, the boiler proved to be safe, and opened up new possibilities. Trevithick realised that his engines need no longer be rooted to the spot; he did not have to build bigger engines to produce more power, simply increase steam pressure.

The next stage was to produce a high-pressure engine mounted on wheels that could be towed along to wherever it was needed. He used a round boiler with an internal flue, that produced steam at about 50psi. The hot gases passed from the firebox, through a U-tube to arrive at the chimney next to the firebox. The exhaust steam from the single cylinder was released through a blast pipe into the chimney, which effectively drew air through the fire. Blast-pipe exhaust would be reinvented a quarter of a century later when Robert Stephenson came to design the famous railway locomotive *Rocket*. Because exhaust steam puffed out at every stroke of the piston, the engines became known as 'Puffers'. The next stage seems obvious now, what if the puffer, instead of working machinery, was used to turn the wheels on which it was mounted? Would that enable it to move itself along? Trevithick conducted a very basic experiment to see if the friction between wheel and ground was sufficient for movement, by turning the wheels of a cart by hand and seeing that it did indeed move. That was all he needed to decide that he would build a steam engine that would move itself, a road locomotive. Once again, a model was built and tried, and only then was he ready to build a full-scale road engine.

In 1801 he designed his first steam road carriage. The boiler and cylinder were cast at the engineering works owned by his father-in-law, Henry Harvey, special parts such as valves were made at the workshop of his friend Andrew Harvey and assembly was the work of a local blacksmith Jonathan Tyack. A contemporary account by a man, known only as 'old Stephen Williams' describes the first outing at Camborne:

> 'In the year 1801, upon Christmas-eve, coming on evening, Captain Dick [Trevithick] got up steam, out in the high-road, we jumped on as many as could, may be seven or eight of us. 'T'was a stiffish hill going from the Wath up to Camborne Beacon, but she went off like a little bird.
>
> 'When she had gone about a quarter of a mile, there was a roughish piece of road covered with loose stones; she didn't go quite so fast, and as it was a flood of rain, and we were very squeezed together, I jumped off. She was going faster than I could walk, and they went up the hill about a quarter or half a mile farther, when they turned her and came back again.'

The actual details of the engine are not accurately known, but at least the overall pattern is clear, and Trevithick's son Francis provided the best information from his own research when writing his father's biography. Like the puffers, the cylindrical boiler had a return flue, the U-shaped tube, so that – unlike the familiar steam engines we see today, the fireman stood at the chimney end of the machine. The single vertical cylinder was embedded in the boiler, and the piston attached to a crosshead. with connecting rods at either end to the drive wheels. Steam was controlled by a simple four-way cock. Apparently, the heat of the fire was increased by mechanical bellows in the first version and not by exhaust blast. When it came to building a replica to celebrate the bicentenary of this remarkable machine, the builders were faced with several problems, one of which was steering. This was by a tiller system attached to the front axle. This was very difficult to control and to make life a bit simpler, a peg board was added, so that the tiller could be held against a suitably positioned peg for going round corners. Even with this device it is hard work keeping everything under control, as anyone who has had the good fortune to travel on the engine can testify. Did the original have such a device? We do not know – but we do know that steering was definitely a problem.

Following the success of the first run, Trevithick and a colleague, Andrew Vivian, decided to form a partnership to develop the engine further. On Boxing Day, the pair of them set of for Tehidy, two miles away to show off the machine to the influential

The 1801 engine had proved that a steam carriage would work and Trevithick went on to design a far grander steam carriage, with which he hoped to impress wealthy investors in London. It failed to attract any backers but again a replica has been built, this time by Tom Brogden. This photograph was taken outside the premises in Leather Lane, Clerkenwell where the bodywork for the original was built on the occasion of the unveiling of a plaque to commemorate the event.

de Dunstanville family, who had encouraged Trevithick in his experiments. Before they got there, they hit a gulley that wrenched the tiller out of Vivian's hand and the engine finished up in a ditch. The two pioneers decided to make the best of a bad job and made their way to the nearby hostelry, abandoning the carriage. Unfortunately, the fire still burned in the grate and, while the two men enjoyed a drink, the whole engine caught fire and the first successful steam locomotive to travel the roads of Britain was reduced to smithereens.

It was not quite the disaster it might have been. The 1801 machine had never been more than a prototype. The next stage was to design a genuine steam carriage that could carry passengers in comfort,

The engine of the London carriage was under the coach, hence the very large wheels needed to lift the body high enough to fit it in. Unlike the coachwork, the engine was constructed in Cornwall.

and it was decided that it would be shown off not in Cornwall but in London, where they hoped to find wealthy customers and investors. They spent a great deal of time preparing their plans, in order to apply for a patent. This was achieved in February 1802 and as a result we have much more knowledge of the engine, as detailed designs had to be lodged at the patent office. Unlike the Camborne engine, the cylinder was horizontal, with once again the steam cylinder embedded in it. The piston rod was forked to allow movement for the crankshaft that drove the immense rear wheels – roughly eight feet in diameter. The whole engine was slung beneath the coach body, built by William Felton of Leather Lane in Clerkenwell, London. It was basically a standard stage coach design, but there was still the tricky problem of steering to deal with. This time, the tiller was attached to a single, small front wheel.

Once again a replica has been built, this time by Tom Brogden of Macclesfield, and in 2003 the machine was brought to Leather Lane, home of the original carriage builder, for the unveiling of a plaque. The author had the pleasant experience of travelling in style in the coach with Frank Trevithick Okuno, a direct descendant of the great engineer. We were driven round Regent's Park, feeling rather like royalty, and were very much the centre of attention. One contemporary description of riding in the carriage made it seem very uncomfortable: a former sea captain declared that it made him feel more seasick than he ever had aboard a ship. There was certainly no discomfort of that sort when travelling in the replica.

The original was given its demonstration run in Oxford Street, which was cleared of traffic for the occasion. Crowds gathered at every vantage point to see the 'Trevithick Dragon'. But curiously, very little if anything was written about it at the time. An account of a trip down Tottenham Court Road with John Vivian, Andrew's brother, probably gives a hint of why investors were not rushing to put in their money:

> 'She was going about five or six miles an hour, and Captain Dick called out, 'Put the helm down, John' and before I could tell what was up, Captain Dick's foot was upon the steering-wheel handle, and we were tearing down six or seven yards of railing from a garden wall. A person put his head from a window, and called out, "What the devil are you doing there! What the devil is that thing!"'

Clearly steering was still a major headache, but whatever the reason, no one showed any interest in future development. The London carriage was to be Trevithick's last attempt to make such a vehicle. The steering problem as such was not solved, but over the next couple of years machines were built that made it irrelevant. Trevithick locomotives would be put on rails and in 1804 he gave the first ever demonstration of a railway locomotive in South Wales. But before that he had set two different ideas into motion. The first was represented by the puffers, his portable steam engine. It was this idea that would eventually lead to the development of the traction engine. The second was the idea of steam carriages for public transport on the roads, and that idea too would be followed up over the next decades, and will be the subject of the next chapter.

CHAPTER TWO

The Steam Omnibus

Trevithick's experimental road vehicles may not have attracted any backers, but they were at least practical machines, even if there were still several problems that remained to be sorted out. Perhaps the most extraordinary feature of the next phase in the attempt to develop road locomotives is that the engineers responsible should ignore such a promising beginning and opt for an entirely different form of motion.

The first of these strange contraptions was designed by William Brunton of the Butterley Iron Works in Derbyshire who took out a patent in 1813 for his 'travelling engine'. In part, it was very conventional, with a cylindrical boiler mounted on four wheels and with a single horizontal cylinder embedded in the boiler. But instead of driving the wheels directly, the piston rod was attached to a long lever that reached down to the ground and acted as an artificial leg. The upper part of this leg was attached to a frame that formed the fulcrum, and was used to activate a second leg. As the piston went in and out, so the legs strolled along, moving the engine. As each step of the legs only moved the 'foot' by 24 inches, the vehicle could hardly be said to sprint along, but rather ambled at a slow walking pace. The engine was actually put to work at the Newbottle Colliery in the north east of England. It was, not surprisingly, unsuccessful, but the company persevered in using it for a few months, until in 1815 the boiler exploded, killing several people.

Amazingly, Brunton was not the only engineer trying to make walking machines. It would appear that in spite of Trevithick's work, there was still a worry that simply turning wheels would not give sufficient grip to move a vehicle.

Another version was designed by David Gordon, a highly respected engineer, and patented in 1824. But before building his walking engine he tried out an even more bizarre machine. Again, the starting point seems very conventional, a four wheeled locomotive. But instead of running on the road it ran inside a nine-foot diameter cylinder. Cogged wheels on the engine engaged with teeth set inside the great hollow drum, which then rolled along, pushing a carriage in front of it. According to the inventor's

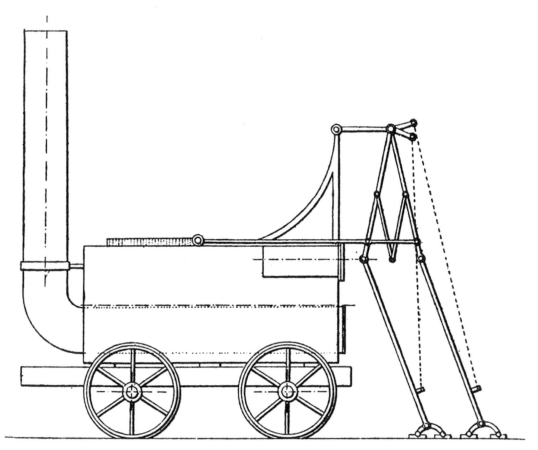

William Brunton's 'Mechanical Traveller' was patented in 1813. In many respects it looks like many other early steam locomotives but in this case the piston rod from the horizontal steam cylinder is attached to a long lever that is joined to form one of the legs that walk the vehicle along. The drawing comes from a French publication *Origine de la Locomotive*.

father, Alexander Gordon, 'it will be obvious that a roller of this kind, so far from deteriorating a road, must materially improve it'. In fact, one could say that it was the very first steam roller, but it was never a success. He then moved on to devise a walking engine, that had, according to the Engineers and Mechanics Encyclopaedia of 1839 two engines, but that simply meant there were two cylinders, one on each side of the vehicle. It was moved along by six legs operated by a crank and connecting rods, in a quite complex system. It was possible to lift the 'feet' off the ground when going downhill for example. It was certainly ingenious but no more successful than Brunton's earlier version. Gordon found that although the machine worked after a fashion, it was still unable to move at anything more than a slow walking pace before

The Shillibeer Omnibus was first introduced to London to take city workers from Paddington station to the Bank of England in 1829. Its popularity owed a great deal to the famously courteous uniformed staff, one of whom is seen here escorting a lady into the broad carriage. The illustration comes from Moore's *Omnibuses and Cabs* 1902.

breaking down. If there was ever going to be any progress in the development of road vehicles, then it was going to have to return to more conventional ideas.

While these somewhat bizarre experiments were being tried with road vehicles, rather better progress was being made with engines set on rails. The early Trevithick engines had worked well enough, but tended to fracture the brittle cast iron rails. The first attempt to overcome the problem was devised for the Middleton Colliery Railway near Leeds, using a rack and pinion system. This made it possible to decrease the weight of the engines without sacrificing tractive power and so preserve the rails. It became, in 1812, the world's first commercially successful steam railway and acted as a huge encouragement to other engineers to develop railway locomotives, George Stephenson among them. He was chief engineer for the first public railway to use steam locomotives, the Stockton & Darlington, opened in 1825. It was mainly built to serve local coal mines but did have a regular passenger service.

Travellers on the railway, however, were not hauled by steam; they still travelled in a conventional coach pulled by horses, the only difference being it was fitted with flanged wheels for running on the rails. Two decades after Trevithick's first experimental coach trundled through the streets of London, passengers whether travelling by road or rail still depended, literally, on horse power.

Progress for steam-powered passenger vehicles may have been slow to virtually non-existent, but there were important changes on urban roads. The idea of building coaches to take large numbers of passengers through city streets dates back to the 1660s, when the first attempt was made, but proved unsuccessful. The real story begins in France, when Jacques Laffitte built an eighteen-seat carriage. One of these vehicles was used by a Monsieur Baudry who ran the vehicle to take customers to his bathing establishment on the edge of Nantes. It was run on a regular timetable and if all the seats were not taken by would-be bathers, the general public could pay a fare and travel as well. It ran past a local grocer's shop called Omnès and, as a pun on the name, an advert appeared for Omnès Omnibus. The name omnibus soon came into general use.

The man who brought the omnibus to Britain was George Shillibeer. Born in London in 1797, he served briefly as a midshipman in the Navy before joining Hatchetts of Long Acre, London to learn the trade of coach building. He moved to Paris in the 1820s, where he designed wide-bodied omnibuses capable of carrying up to 24 passengers inside the coach. They proved very popular and in 1827 he was approached by a Quaker girls' school in Stoke Newington, asking him to provide a coach for the girls. So Shillibeer can be said to be the first person to build a school bus. It was perhaps the success of this vehicle that gave him the idea of returning to London to set up an omnibus service, running to a regular timetable with designated 'bus stops' in London.

The first Shillibeer omnibus went into service on 4 July 1829, between the Bank of England and Paddington; the latter was then merely a suburb, for the railway would only arrive some years later. There were four services a day in each direction, and passengers paid a shilling for the full distance and sixpence for travelling part of the way. The vehicles looked very attractive, with highly decorative paintwork and were manned by smartly uniformed staff. All the passengers were carried on the inside, unlike the existing coaches where only the wealthy enjoyed that privilege. The bus was not

THE 'ENTERPRISE' STEAM OMNIBUS
Built by Mr. Walter Hancock, of Stratford, for the
LONDON AND PADDINGTON STEAM CARRIAGE COMPANY
— Commenced Running April 22nd 1833 —

Walter Hancock's steam omnibus *Enterprise* built for the London and Paddington Steam Carriage Company. It carried sixteen passengers and worked on the same London route as the Shillibeer. Although it ran a very successful service, the Company mistreated the inventor, who lost almost £1,000 on the venture.

necessarily very comfortable, with narrow bench seats, but was immediately popular; the *Morning Post* of 7 July 1829 was enthusiastic:

'Saturday the new vehicle, called the Omnibus, commenced running from Paddington to the City, and excited considerable notice, both from the novel form of the carriage, and the elegance with which it is fitted out. It is capable of accommodating 16 or 18 persons, all inside, and we apprehend it would be almost impossible to make it overturn, owing to the great width of the carriage. It was drawn by three beautiful bays abreast, after the French fashion. The Omnibus is a handsome machine, in the shape of a van. The width the horses occupy will render the vehicle rather inconvenient to be turned or driven through some of the streets of London.'

The width of the Shillibeer was indeed a problem, but it did suggest the idea that a steam omnibus might prove rather more useful than the steam stage coach developed by Trevithick. Two names are outstanding in the next stage of development; Walter Hancock and Goldsworthy Gurney, but neither was first in the field.

In 1821, Julius Griffith of Brompton, Middlesex, designed a steam powered coach and had it built by one of the foremost engineers of the day, Joseph Bramah. It was a curious vehicle, consisting of a flat frame mounted on four wheels, above which was the actual carriage, very like a stage coach carriage, mounted on springs. The engine and boiler were placed above the rear axle and the rear wheels were driven through intermediate gearing. The boiler had horizontal water and steam tubes. The steering was via a steering wheel at the front of the platform. It was nevertheless given an enthusiastic reception in the twopenny weekly newspaper Limbard's *Mirror*. Oddly, given that the machine was clearly intended for passengers, it was discussed solely in terms of freight. It ended by saying that if it could carry goods at a rate of 5mph and travel for twenty hours a day at a cost 25 per cent below current rates for carriage, 'there can be no question that he will have deserved well of his country and of mankind'. The paper also included an engraving of the carriage. But in the event the boiler proved to be totally inadequate for the job in hand. As a result, the machine made a few experimental runs at the factory, never took to the road and was then largely forgotten. It does, however, seem to have been seen by Walter Hancock and helped to enthuse him with the idea of developing a steam carriage of his own.

Hancock was born in Marlborough, Wiltshire, where his father was a timber merchant and cabinetmaker. He originally trained as a watchmaker and jeweller, an occupation that would have involved him in acquiring skills in the use of a variety of machine tools. He was eventually to begin his own business, but his life was to change dramatically, thanks to his brother Thomas. Thomas Hancock became interested in rubber, a substance that had begun to find limited use in Britain in the eighteenth century, but it proved a very wasteful process, with large quantities of small off cuts going to waste. He wondered if it would be possible to recombine them to make them usable. At first, he tried treating the rubber with chemicals and when that failed decided mechanical means might be better, and devised a machine for amalgamating them – the masticator. It worked, and he established a factory in London. But he also needed some means of making his machinery, and he turned to his brother Walter, who was the experienced mechanic in the family. Walter found premises in Stratford, East London and worked for Thomas as a subcontractor. With his own workshop, he had freedom to develop his ideas and he began experimenting with a new type of steam engine.

Instead of the usual arrangement of cylinder and piston, steam was passed to a pair of stout but flexible bags, made of layers of canvas bonded together by rubber solution and able to withstand a pressure up to 60psi. The bags were alternately filled with steam and exhausted. Having studied Julius Griffith's machine Hancock considered building a steam carriage himself, in the belief that his engine, much lighter than a conventional engine of iron and brass, would be perfect for transport. It too failed, mainly because it lacked the necessary power, due in large measure to a poorly designed boiler. His next step was described in his own book *Narrative of Twelve Years Experience, 1824-36, Demonstrative of the Practicality and Advantages of Employing Steam Carriages on Common Roads* (1836); hardly a catchy title, but it does make it quite clear what the reader will find in its pages. Slightly confusingly he speaks of himself in the third person:

> 'When once the mind however has been much exercised towards a certain point, it is no easy matter to apply it in a different direction; at least it proved so in this case. Although his experiments demonstrated the inefficiency of his new engine as a locomotive agent, they left on his mind a strong conviction, that the application of steam power to the propulsion of carriages on common roads was decidedly a practical object. The great and essential desideratum seemed to him to be – a boiler that while it should generate steam rapidly, and produce a sufficient and continuous supply, should occupy but little space, be of small weight (comparatively speaking), harmless if it should burst, simple in its construction and inexpensive in its manufacture; to construct such a boiler became now, therefore, his chief study.'

The new boiler consisted of a set of narrow, flat water chambers arranged vertically with iron stays between them. The arrangement was designed to increase the surface area of the water chambers in contact with the hot gases from the fire. It was a remarkably efficient system; with approximately 85 square feet of heating surface exposed to the heat from a grate of just 6 square feet, it was

able to evaporate ten pounds of water while burning just one pound of coke. The fuel was chosen because it was smokeless, an important consideration if it was to be used in an engine trundling through crowded city streets. Hancock produced a number of improvements over the years, including an arrangement that allowed fire bars clogged with clinker to be pulled out, while at the same time a new set was pulled in by a rack and pinion to replace them. There was never any need to drop the fire. One of the most significant features of the Hancock boiler was its safety, as he himself explained, quoting an actual example:

> 'I was travelling about nine miles an hour at the time, the boiler was the twenty-fourth part of an inch thick. I was working then at 100 lbs on the square inch, with thirteen persons on the vehicle, and all of a sudden the carriage stopped – for what purpose I was at a loss to know. I got from my steerage seat, and went to the engineer to ask him what was the reason he had stopped the steam? He told me he had not stopped the carriage and he

A modern working replica of the Hancock omnibus, built by Tom Brogden, who was also responsible for the replica of Trevithick's London carriage. It provides a surprisingly smooth and comfortable ride.

immediately applied his hand to the gauge cocks and found there was neither steam nor water in the boiler. I immediately knew that the boiler had burst. They (the passengers) said they did not know it as they heard no noise. I told them I did not mean they should know it. I said that I would show them it was so; and I took the boiler from the carriage and unscrewed it, and there were four large holes that I could put my hand into. This occurred from the chambers being too thin, all the water was driven out of the boiler and yet there was no injury to any person, there was not one person that heard any report, there was no steam and there were no symptoms in any way that the machine itself had burst.'.

The carriage with the burst boiler was the *Infant*. It was not the first engine he built after abandoning the rubberised bags. That was a three-seater reminiscent of the old Cugnot engine, in that the front wheel was used both for steering and was also driven by a pair of oscillating cylinders set to either side of it. It was not a great success, and the next carriage, the *Infant II*, was very different – a four wheel vehicle with ten seats. The engine was now placed at the back of the carriage and had a chain drive to the back axle. There was still one odd feature; the engine had two oscillating cylinders that were soon to prove troublesome. So, the *Infant* was reborn, this time as a fourteen-seater open-topped charabanc and with the oscillating cylinders replaced by a fixed vertical engine. The drive was still by chain, protected by an under shield from the mud and grit thrown up from the road. The coach originally went into service between London and Brighton, but the London and Brighton Steam Carriage Company that was formed in 1832 was never able to go into business. Instead the improved *Infant* made several trips for hire from its base in Stratford, East London.

Hancock continued to build carriages, largely based on the *Infant* of which the best known is *Enterprise*. This was a fourteen-seater omnibus built for the London and Paddington Steam Carriage Company, designed for the same route as the Shillibeers. There was a clear understanding that *Enterprise* would make a series of trial runs and if those were satisfactory, the company would order more vehicles. With Hancock himself in charge of the bus, it made regular runs between Paddington and Bank over a period of sixteen days, and unlike the wide-bodied horse omnibuses had no difficulty navigating through the London streets and was reported as having reached speeds of 16mph.

The experiment was declared a success and the omnibus duly purchased, but instead of ordering more vehicles, *Enterprise* was handed over to the company's engineer, who dismantled it and built his own version, including minor modifications, not so much as improvements, more to avoid piracy charges. The new version proved hopelessly inferior, and there was justice of a sort. The piratical company failed and Hancock was able to buy back his omnibus – though he lost a considerable amount of money on the deal. *Enterprise* continued to be run for a number of years and now runs again, or at least a replica does. Built by Tom Brogden, who

A view inside the *Enterprise* replica, showing the vertical two-cylinder engine.

was also responsible for Trevithick's London carriage replica, it was constructed using Hancock's original plans and drawings. As with other replicas of early steam vehicles, it is fascinating to see it in motion – and to be impressed by just how well it performs.

Hancock went on to build further vehicles, including *Erin* that was sent for trials in Dublin, but seemingly the Irish were unimpressed, and it was returned to London, where it joined the developing Hancock fleet of vehicles. Another abortive order came for a steam bus for Vienna, but before the work had been completed, the Viennese decided that they did not want a steam omnibus after all, and asked for the machine to be shortened, so that it could be used to pull carriages. They then declared that they would not actually pay for the alterations and eventually the order was cancelled. The machine never left the country, but was converted instead into a 22-seat charabanc and named *Automaton*. It was similar to a slightly smaller earlier vehicle, which had the seemingly daunting name *Autopsy*. The original definition of the word is, literally, 'seeing with our own eyes' or in this case when people doubted the whole notion of steam vehicles 'seeing is believing'. At that date, it had nothing to do with chopping up dead bodies!

Hancock ran many services around London, and on one memorable occasion the most powerful of the vehicles, *Automaton*, took the Stratford cricket team and a party of supporters to Epping for a match, a total of 32 passengers, together with the three crew. There were attempts to make even more ambitious journeys, with demonstration runs to Marlborough in the west and out to Birmingham. However, services were mainly restricted to the London area, going to and fro from the suburbs to the City.

The other equally famous pioneer of steam vehicles was Goldsworthy Gurney. His carriages became so well known that they were even the subject of a satirical poem. It has been attributed to Thomas Hood, but if it was his work then that skilful wordsmith was definitely having an off day:

'Instead of journeys, people now
May travel on a Gurney,
With Steam to do the horses' work
By Pow'r of Attorney.
Tho'with a load
It may explode.
And you'll find yourself quite undone;

Travelling fast to Heav'ns Gates
Instead of down to London.'

Gurney was born in Cornwall in 1793, and in his early years, while still a schoolboy at Truro Grammar School, was introduced to Richard Trevithick and became interested in his experiments with steam vehicles. However, it was to be some time before he became personally involved in steam experiments. Instead he studied medicine with Dr. Avery of Wadebridge and eventually took over his practice. After his marriage in 1814 he moved to London, where he not only had a thriving practice but also gave lectures in chemistry. In 1822 he was appointed lecturer in chemistry at the Surrey Institution, a body that had been set up in 1808 to promote scientific studies. He worked on many different scientific projects, from chemistry to electrical studies and even devised a strange musical instrument, not unlike a glass harmonica. It was during his scientific studies that he began experiments with steam jets that led him to consider how to devise an efficient steam carriage.

Considering that Gurney had seen Trevithuick's early experiments, it is odd to find that when he started to think about building a steam carriage, he began by trying to construct a 'walking' machine with mechanical legs, but that was the orthodoxy of the time:

'it was at this time a general opinion, and the fact was stated to me by eminent engineers, as 'settled by actual experiment', that if the power of any engine was applied to the wheels of a carriage on which it was mounted, with a view to propelling it along a common road, the wheels would turn round on the ground without moving the carriage forward. In explanation this effect was referred to the periphery of the wheel not having sufficient hold on the ground to make an available fulcrum. This came from such high authority, that I looked on it as a settled axiom in mechanics.'

However, he soon abandoned the project and settled for the more conventional idea of driving wheels. He designed a new type of tubular boiler, described in M.A. Alderson's *Essay on the Nature and Application of Steam* 1834:

'the tubes being about 1½ or 2 inches in diameter, were bent in such a way that the bottom series formed the grate-bars of the fire while they were returned over the fire in another series, and ended in a cylindrical receiver for the steam.'

The boiler was tested up to 200psi. but in service rarely exceeded 100psi. It was, like the Hancock boiler, comparatively safe, as a fracture of one of the tubes would not cause an explosion. It was, however, prone to priming with water being carried over from the boiler along with the steam. It was less efficient than the Hancock, evaporating just 5 lb. of water for each pound of coke, just half of that achieved by the latter. Francis Maceroni, the son of an Italian merchant living in Manchester and a former Colonel of Cavalry, serving the King of Naples, came to work with Gurney in developing a steam carriage. He also persuaded friends to invest in the enterprise. The first experiments, with a small model powered by ammonia gas, were sufficiently successful for Gurney to hire a workshop in Oxford Street, where he built his first full-sized carriage. When that was successful, he was able to take out a patent in 1825 and begin manufacturing at new premises in Albany Street near Regent's Park.

Maceroni did not last long in the concern:

'having long been thoroughly convinced of the incapacity of Mr. Gurney's boiler and machinery, I abandoned all thoughts of the business and went to Constantinople to serve the Mussulmans against the Russians'.

He would return to steam later, when he became even more scathing about Gurney's efforts, arguing that he himself could never have succeeded 'had I been foolish enough to copy any of his miserable pretended mechanical "arrangements", or his still more miserable boiler.' As he was equally damning in his comments on Hancock's carriage, one might reasonably assume that in his view, no one had ever done anything worth commending until he himself started designing steam carriages. We shall see shortly whether or not his claims were justified.

Gurney built a fourteen-seater coach with a two-cylinder engine, driving a cranked axle. There was also an auxiliary engine to work the feed-water pump and the fan blower for the fire. Rather alarmingly, there were no brakes, but the steerer could control both steam valve and the reversing handle. The actual steering mechanism was different from that used by Hancock; where he

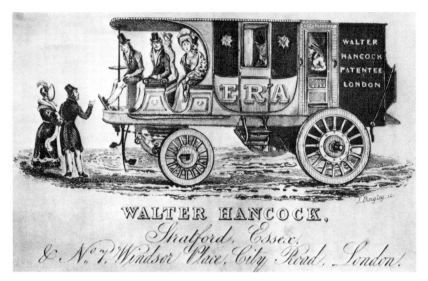

Hancock's *Era* was renamed *Erin* and taken to Dublin but after eight weeks of demonstration runs, there was no interest. Eventually it was to be one of three steam vehicles running successfully in London for five months in 1856.

used a system for turning the front axle, Gurney mounted his coach on four wheels, but had a pair of much smaller pilot wheels in front of it for steering. It was successful and was said to have run a round trip between London and Bath at an average speed of 15mph. But as Anthony Bird explained in his book *Roads and Vehicles* 1969, although such a speed was possible it was very far from being an average. On the trial run from the capital to Bath and back again, the engine actually broke down on the outward journey, and on the return achieved the required speed on just one section of the route. Apart from the actual travelling time, there also had to be stops to replenish the water tank.

He later changed the design altogether. Instead of a composite engine and coach, he built a separate traction unit, the steam drag that pulled the coach behind it. One reason for the change was the nervousness of potential passengers, scared by the notion of sitting on top of a high-pressure boiler. Possibly they had read the poem quoted earlier in the chapter. It was, of course, a much lighter vehicle than the omnibus, and it could even have been one of these vehicles that attempted the 15mph run, unencumbered by coach and passengers.

At least half a dozen drags were built and went into service. The most successful route was run by Sir Charles Dance, who also contributed to the design by suggesting modifications to the boiler.

He ran four coaches a day between Cheltenham and Gloucester from 21 February 1831 to 22 June of that year. The omnibus trailer carried sixteen passengers and it proved very popular, largely because the fares were half those of the stage coaches. But there was inevitable opposition, both from the owners of horse-drawn coaches and from the Turnpike Trusts, who were responsible for the upkeep of the roads. The first obviously hated the new opposition and the latter feared extra repair costs. Towards the end of the series of runs, the road was covered with large stones, taken by Gurney as a deliberate attempt at sabotage, which resulted in three crank axles being broken. Equally seriously a new set of toll charges was introduced, penalising the steam carriages. The example of the local Trust was soon followed by other authorities. Charges for coaches were reasonably standard, ranging from just 4 to 5 shillings for a

Goldsworthy Gurney made several attempts to build steam vehicles, including an early version with walking legs, similar to Brunton's, before eventually settling on the steam drag, essentially a tractor that could haul a coach behind it. The working replica is seen going through its paces.

coach and four horses but steamer charges were far higher; that on the Liverpool to Prescot road was set at a staggering £2 – 8 –0. for a journey of no more than a dozen miles. Sir Charles Dance withdrew the Gloucester-Cheltenham service.

Gurney pressed Parliament to insist on a fairer toll system, but with little effect until 1834, when the Commons passed a toll relief bill, only to have it thrown out in the Lords. By this time Maceroni had returned from the wars and built his own steam carriage that went into service between Paddington and Edgware. It was not a success, but as he had patents in both Belgium and France he arranged for two steamers to be sent to France. He left it to an Italian speculator Colonel d'Asda to show off the carriages, which he did to such good effect that he sold them both and absconded with the proceeds. That brought Maceroni's venture to an close. The first days of steam travel by road were coming to an end.

Gurney lost a considerable amount of money in developing the steam carriage and in 1831 he returned to Cornwall, where he developed a new form of artificial lighting that was to be used eventually in the House of Commons. He also designed a new, efficient heating stove and the Gurney stove can still be seen in some of Britain's larger churches and cathedrals. He was eventually knighted for his pioneering efforts in heating and lighting – not for his work on steam carriages.

John Scott Russell is best known for his work as a ship builder, but he also invented steam carriages and ran them successfully for some time. In appearance, it was not dissimilar to Trevithick's London carriage, being very much in the stage coach mode, but the mechanism was quite different. There were two cylinders, each of which was connected via crossheads and side rods to two separate crankshafts. Each unit had its own clutch, so that one could be disengaged when cornering. The connection between the engine and the crankshaft was via spur wheels, with a 2:1 ratio. Exhaust steam was passed to the tall chimney, providing an extra blast to the fire – the system used in Trevithick's early railway locomotives and brought back into use in Stephenson's *Rocket.* A tender was towed behind the coach, carrying coke and water.

Six of these vehicles were built in Edinburgh for the Steam Carriage Company of Scotland. They were used to run a regular service between Glasgow and Paisley, often carrying as many as thirty or forty passengers at a time; six inside the coach and the rest finding whatever space was available on the outside. The journey

This 1828 cartoon by Henry Alkens shows how he imagines traffic might be in the Whitechapel Road in 1830 with a wonderfully unlikely array of steam carriages. The original appeared in *Punch*.

took just over half an hour, but once clear of the restrictions of Glasgow streets, the carriage was said to bowl along at a very respectable seventeen miles an hour. The service was popular with the passengers, but not with the authorities responsible for the upkeep of the roads. They tried to stop the service by piling loose stones over the surface. It did not stop the carriages from running, but may well have contributed to a fatal accident. A wheel broke, the carriage fell over and ruptured the boiler. After that the coaches were banned by the courts and the experiment came to an end.

There was always strong opposition to the whole idea of steam carriages, but Sir Charles Dance made an eloquent case on their behalf in a letter to Gurney:

'Obstacles are always thrown in the way of a new invention particularly if it is likely to produce important results from the prejudices of those who have not fairly examined its merits and by the opposition of others who expect their interests will be effected by its success. Thus objections have been made to these carriages by various descriptions of persons, viz. country gentlemen, trustees of roads, farmers, coach proprietors, coachmen, post boys, etc. Some said they would be injurious to agriculture, others that they would destroy the roads, others that removing horses would ruin the farmers and others that it would ruin the coach proprietors and throw all the hands employed by them out of work. To these I replied that the land which is used to keep one horse would keep eight people and consequently that the removal of one thousand horses would feed eight thousand people. That the cheap and expeditious mode of conveying passengers and carrying everything to market would eminently tend to the welfare of all classes agricultural and commercial, that the roads would suffer less injury from the broad wheels of steamers than from horses feet and the narrow wheels of the present stage coaches, that coach proprietors would get more custom by carrying people at half the present prices and would require less capital than in the present uncertain outlay for horses, that coachmen, postboys and horsekeepers would also be benefitted as more men are employed about a steam coach than a horse coach, in addition to the increased employment of artificers.'

The arguments may have been sound, but they failed to convince the opponents, especially the highway authorities, who continued to impose punitive tolls and restrictions on steam carriages. Even if they had not it is doubtful if investment in steam road carriages would have been popular; Britain was to enter a period that became known as the years of Railway Mania. Everyone wanted railway shares and scrambled and fought to get hold of the latest issue, even if some of those lines were unlikely ever to show a profit or, indeed, get built at all. If there were to a place for the self-propelled steam vehicle that did not run on rails that it would have to come from a new source.

CHAPTER THREE

Down on the Farm

The Industrial Revolution of eighteenth century Britain was matched by an equally important Agricultural Revolution; indeed, it could be argued that without the latter, the former could never have occurred. A population moving from country to town had to be fed and in order for that to happen productivity had to be improved. That, inevitably, involved a degree of mechanisation. One particularly arduous part of farm work was threshing, separating the grain from the straw and chaff. The work was still being done, as it had been for thousands of years, by beating the harvested crop with flails. The work was not merely hard, but dangerously unhealthy; the effect on the lungs of the flying dust from the flails in a confined room is not difficult to imagine. The first attempts at mechanisation was a device invented by Michael Menzies in Scotland in 1732, that simply replaced flails worked by human muscle power by flails mounted on a drum, worked by a water wheel. It was not a success. A second method involved pulling the grain through a comb, then rubbing it in a device like the familiar corn mill. This also proved unsatisfactory. It was a Scottish millwright, Andrew Meikle, who finally solved the problem when he built his threshing machine in 1786.

The Meikle threshing machine consisted of a metal or wooden drum, rotating rapidly against a concave surface, with just a small gap between the two. The grain was fed in from above and the rubbing action separated the grain from the chaff. It was later improved by the addition of 'straw arms', spiked rollers that pulled away the straw, allowing the grain and chaff to fall onto a shaker that completed the work of separation. These were bulky machines that needed a suitable power source. A few were worked by water wheels, but this was very expensive, and many farms would not even have had a suitable watercourse. The more common method was the horse mill, worked by horses walking round a circular track to turn a shaft to work the machine. This required a special building as well as the machinery. The agriculturist Arthur Young in his review of agriculture in Oxfordshire, published in 1813, noted that Lord Macclesfield had

The threshing machines in use in the nineteenth century were based on the original design by Andrew Meikle of 1786, in which the grain was removed by being passed between a rotating drum and a concave plate. This more sophisticated version was built by Garrett's in the 1850s.

built a four-horse threshing mill and it had cost him £120. That is the equivalent of nearly £80,000 today. It was an expense that only the richest farmers could afford. The other alternative was to use a high-pressure steam engine.

Richard Trevithick had envisaged his portable steam engine as being used mainly in the industry he knew best, mining, but was the first to see the opportunity of applying it in agriculture. He designed an engine to work a threshing machine for Sir Christopher Hawkins of Trethewin in Cornwall in 1812. It was a simple machine with a 9-inch cylinder and a flywheel that also carried the rope drive to the threshing machine. It worked at 30 strokes a minute and turned the threshing drum at

360 revolutions per minute and he claimed it would do the work of a four-horse mill. He estimated the total cost at £90 that compared very favourably with the £120 of the horse mill, and running costs were estimated to be a good deal lower: 2s 6d (12.5p) per day for steam against £1 a day for horses. To prove his point, he gave a demonstration in front of independent witnesses, who produced a wholly favourable report:

> 'We hereby certify that a fire was lighted under the boiler of the engine five minutes after eight o'clock, and at twenty-five minutes after nine the thrashing mill began to work, in which time 1 bushel of coal was consumed. That from the time the mill began to work to two minutes after two o'clock, being four hours and three-quarters, 1500 sheaves of barley were thrashed clean, and 1 bushel of coal more was consumed. We think there was sufficient steam remaining in the boiler to have thrashed from 50 to 100 sheaves more barley, and the water in the boiler was by no means exhausted. We had the satisfaction to observe that a common labourer regulated the thrashing mill, and in a moment of time made it go faster, slower, or entirely to cease working.'

Not only was the Trevithick mill cheaper than the horse mill, but it proved far more efficient. A direct comparison with the horse mill described by Young, showed the Trevithick engine treating 316 sheaves a day against 258 for the horse mill. Trevithick was soon advertising his new engine in the *Royal Cornish Gazette.* It may have been cheaper but it was still far too expensive for most farmers. However, the case for working different types of agricultural machinery had been made. Trevithick started receiving orders for machines to work sugar mills in the West Indies, and others soon followed his lead. A lucrative market was on the cotton plantations of the Southern States of America, where Eli Whitney's 'gin' had been introduced. This was used to separate the cotton fibres from the seeds of the plant – and soon the Americans were making their own engines. A survey carried out in Louisiana in 1818 recorded no fewer than 274 engines in use. But, like the British engines, they were expensive. A Louisiana planter was advertising 12 horsepower engines at $2500 each. The price was still far beyond the means of many.

Richard Trevithick was the first to apply steam to threshing. His simple engine had a 9-inch diameter cylinder and a flywheel that carried a rope drive to the threshing drum. It turned the drum at 360 revolutions per minute and was said to do the work of four horses. The engine is now preserved in the Science Museum, London.

Developments were not, however, limited to Britain. In America Jerome Increase Case imported half a dozen rather crude 'Ground Hog' threshing machines that he used for a time in New York State. Recognising that there was a far greater area of grain being cultivated further west, he moved to Rochester, Wisconsin. He sold five of his machines and worked with just the one remaining.

It was in Rochester that he met Richard Ela who sold fanning machines for separating grain. Case realised that a far more efficient machine could be built by combing the beating of the Ground Hog with fanning, and once he had completed his prototype, he moved to Racine, where he established a water-powered factory. The machine, introduced in 1847, was a success, but originally had to be powered either by water or some form of tread mill. Case soon realised that an alternative form of power was needed, and inevitably turned to steam. It was the start of what was to become one of America's most important manufacturers of steam-powered machinery for agriculture.

Back in Britain, development was slow, since so few could afford the expense of installing expensive machinery that would only be used for a few weeks each year. There was, however, another possibility available to the farmer. If the threshing machine was mounted on wheels, the same machine could be taken to a number of different farms, provided there was a suitable power source available. And, of course, by the beginning of the nineteenth century there was: the portable steam engine, the Trevithick puffer. He began offering puffers at £65 each, still a lot of money, but because they were portable it was possible for a group of farmers to get together and purchase a machine that they could share, moving it from farm to farm. Alternatively, anyone with the necessary capital could buy an engine and threshing machine, and take them round the district at harvest time. This was to prove the way forward, but development was slow.

There were many possible reasons why portable engines and threshing machines failed to become an immediate success. Farming was essentially a very conservative industry, and many farms were quite isolated. It was rare for country people to travel far from their own homes, which slowed the spread of new ideas. Manufacturers failed to see a big enough market to go into production and engineers who were interested in developing steam power had other fields that looked far more profitable: the rapidly developing railway system, the ship building industry and providing power for heavy industry. One family concern, however, decided to make the effort.

The story begins with Robert Ransome, a brass and iron founder who moved from Norwich to Ipswich in 1789 to start manufacturing agricultural implements. As a result of a fortuitous accident, he discovered a new method of hardening iron for ploughshares,

The advertisement contrasts the old methods of threshing with the advantages obtained from using one of their portable engines. At the top, men beat the grain with flails; at the bottom is an unlikely scene of treading the grain with teams of galloping horses, while in the centre the corn is being fed from the stack into the threshing drum, powered by steam.

a process that became known as 'chilled casting'. He was able to turn out a new product – the 'self-sharpening' ploughshare. The business prospered and he took his eldest son Robert into partnership in 1809. The younger son, James Allen, was put in charge of a branch of the business in Suffolk, but in 1839 he returned to Ipswich, and a new company was formed – J.R. & A. Ransome.

A factor that needed to be addressed urgently was that of making farmers aware of what new ideas and devices were available. One man who spoke ardently in favour of steam power was

A rare photograph from the early twentieth century showing a portable engine, with its engineer standing to the right with his hand resting on a wheel. The drive to the threshing drum is via the leather belt round the flywheel.

John Lathbury, who went around the country making speeches extolling the virtues of steam threshing. One of those speeches was quoted at length in the *Farmer's Magazine* in 1844. Among the many advantages he spelled out one was perhaps not very tactfully put, since he was speaking in Burton-on-Trent, the heart of the brewing industry; he pointed out that the steam engine took the hard labour out of threshing, so there would be no need to spend a fortune on beer for the labourers. As well as individual propagandists for steam on the farm, a new institution also helped to raise awareness. There were a number of organisations promoting the arts and sciences, and in 1839, farming got its own body, the Royal Agricultural Society. The highlights of the year were the shows where the latest equipment could be put on display and demonstrated. In 1841 the show was held in London and Ransome's decided it was sufficiently important to bring an engine all the way from Ipswich for the event. It offered something very new.

Unlike earlier portable engines, this one was able to move itself. It had a rather cumbersome device, a sprocket on the drive shaft connected with one of the rear wheels. It no longer needed a horse to pull it along, but the company had not yet worked out how to steer the engine, so it still had shafts for a horse and where the horse went the engine would follow.

Ransome's now got more ambitious. The threshing machine still had to be brought to the farm, so why not incorporate that with the power source and make a hybrid – a threshing machine and steam engine combined? This too was presented to the Royal Agricultural Society who declared it a resounding success and awarded it one of their top medals for the year. It was not, however, a commercial success. So Ransome's went back to improving their original engine, this time doing away with the guiding horse by introducing a steering system. It was given a suitably encouraging name 'The Farmer's Friend' and was displayed at the Royal Show in 1849. In the event it turned out to be underpowered and unable to work the threshing machine. It was left to others to take new developments further, though Ransome's would continue to manufacture engines for many years to come.

Thomas Aveling had a modest start in life. At some time around 1836 at the age of twelve he was apprenticed to a farmer, Edward Lake, in Kent. He was later to marry Lake's niece. It soon became apparent that he was more interested in the implements that worked the land than in working the land itself. He was kept busy repairing machinery on the farm and was soon in demand from neighbouring farmers to help them out as well. The path ahead now began to seem clear. In 1856 his father-in-law, Robert Lake, helped him buy a small millwrighting business at Rochester. It was to be the beginning of an outstanding engineering career, in which he was to make a number of major advances in the use of steam power on the roads.

Aveling had seen portable engines in the fields and was not impressed:

'It is an insult to mechanical science, to see half a dozen horses drag along a steam engine, and the sight of six sailing vessels towing a steamer would certainly not be more ridiculous'.

He resolved to solve the ridiculous situation himself, and ordered a portable engine from the Lincoln firm of Clayton and Shuttleworth, founded by Nathaniel Clayton and Joseph Shuttleworth in 1842 as a foundry, initially making cast iron pipes for water supply. They produced their first portable engine in 1845. As soon as Aveling got his engine, he set about adapting it by adding a chain drive, linking the crankshaft to the rear axle. The system worked well enough, but he still had the problem that, because it was designed to be pulled by horses, there was no steering mechanism. In his first trials, he did what Ransome had done: used a horse for steering – at least it was just one horse not the half dozen that had so infuriated him. But it was certainly not meeting his ambition of creating an entirely self-contained engine. So, he replaced the horse with a single wheel added at the front of the engine, which could be steered by a tiller, operated by a man perched just ahead of the boiler.

Tiller steering had proved difficult from the very first steam carriage built by Trevithick. The roads at the time were not exactly smooth, and one can easily imagine the tiller being jerked from the steerer's hands if the engine hit a severe bump or rut; not to mention the fact that the unfortunate man at the front seems to have had a most precarious position. Aveling took his new design to Clayton and Shuttleworth and they were sufficiently impressed to put it into production. Their engines, unlike Ransome's, were powerful enough to do productive work in the fields and proved quite successful, though it must have been obvious that some

A Ruston & Proctor portable engine; the tall chimney is hinged so that it can be lowered for passing under bridges when being towed to the site.

better form of steering would be needed in the future. It was in fact sufficiently successful for many to refer to Aveling, as 'the father of the traction engine'.

Others were also working at developing traction engines at much the same time as Aveling. But where Aveling came to the subject almost by accident, from his farm apprenticeship, the Garrett family had a long history of metal working in Suffolk. It can be slightly confusing, as all the main characters shared the same forename – they were all called Richard. The first notable member was born in 1757, and he was the first to set up business in Leiston, which was to remain the manufacturing centre for as long as the firm remained in business. He retired in 1805, leaving his son, the next Richard, to take over the forge, mainly making sickles and still employing less than a dozen workmen. He married Sarah Balls, the daughter of John Balls. This was a turning point in the development of the family business, for Balls had invented a new type of very efficient threshing machine that had an open drum and beater bars. It was to become the standard model and they began to manufacture the new machines. The company grew until by the time of Richard's death in 1837, the workforce had grown to sixty employees.

The third Richard Garrett was to introduce vital changes to the company. He began manufacturing portable steam engines in 1847 and in 1851 he was able to exhibit them in the Great Exhibition in the Crystal Palace in Hyde Park. Garrett's were not the only company displaying portable engines, and they all attracted a great deal of attention. A contemporary account described their introduction as 'the most remarkable feature in the agricultural operations of the present day', noting that until their arrival threshing machines had not been introduced because of the 'non efficiency of horse power'. Garrett visited the exhibition himself, but what most impressed him were the new ideas on show from America. In agriculture, there was the McCormick reaper, which even if it was intended for use with horses not steam engines represented a very different machine from anything then available in Europe. But what he found even more interesting was nothing to do with agriculture at all: the armoury section.

Robbins and Lawrence of Windsor, Vermont, had sent over half a dozen of the rifles they had manufactured for the US Army. They were awarded a medal and, more importantly for the company, received an order for both machine tools and weapons from the British government. What set them apart from other weapons of the period

This fine nineteenth century drawing shows a typical scene with a portable engine driving the threshing machine and the corn being pitchforked from the stack onto a conveyor to the threshing drum.

was the system used in their manufacture. Robbins and Lawrence had built a brand new factory, complete with precision machine tools, many of them to their own design. With this in place, they were able to produce identical parts, which could then be assembled into finished weapons. It made no difference in what order the different parts were actually made; each individual piece was identical to the other. This made it possible to introduce a rudimentary form of assembly line. Garrett was so impressed with the idea that he decided to go to America to see this new efficient system for himself. On his return, he set about putting what he had learned into practice.

Back in Britain in 1853, Garrett began constructing a new factory at Leiston: the 'Long Shop', also known rather fancifully as 'The Cathedral'. A tall brick building with few distinguishing external features apart from a little bell tower, its true nature is only revealed when you step inside. There is one immense open space, and one can see where the cathedral idea came from. In the centre is a wide, open aisle, with nine bays to either side. Above the bays are two wooden galleries, stretching the full length of the building. The whole was organised so that parts from the machine tools in the bays could be brought to the centre aisle for assembly, and also lowered down from the galleries via a gantry. The engine was slowly moved down the centre aisle, until it was completed and could leave the factory. It was an early attempt to produce a rational assembly-line type of production and represented a major step forward in engineering production practice. The Long Shop is now a steam museum, with Garrett engines among the exhibits.

Garrett began looking at ways of converting the portable engine into what was then known as a 'self moving portable' in 1863. He was far from alone in seeing the advantages of turning the portable into a genuine traction engine. Aveling has already been mentioned and other companies such as John Fowler of Leeds and Charles Burrell of Thetford also began developing engines. There were still numerous problems to overcome, not least the system for transmitting the driving force. Most early manufacturers used chain drive, which was never very satisfactory, largely because chain making itself was in many ways still little more than a cottage industry. Many chains were manufactured in tiny workshops in backyards in the Midlands, with a great concentration in Dudley. The piece workers were sent regular supplies of metal rods that they would heat, bend and

Portable engines were exhibited at the Great Exhibition at the Crystal Palace in 1851. This example was manufactured by Hornsby. The photograph appeared in the official catalogue for the exhibition.

Thomas Aveling is often referred to as the 'Father of the traction engine' as he was the first to convert the horse-drawn portable engine into an engine that moved itself by steam power. The earliest version still used a horse for steering, but was later replaced by the system shown here, in which a man sat in front of the boiler steered by means of a tiller attached to the single front wheel.

weld together. It was not easy to get uniformity and chain drive could literally fail through a weak link.

The obvious solution was to have a system not dissimilar to that already in use on the railways; where a connecting rod from the piston was attached either to a crank or a cranked axle. The first engineer to apply the connection through gears was William Bray of Folkestone. He was an ingenious man, who also came up with a device that allowed engines to work on soft ground, which he thought would make them suitable for replacing horses for ploughing. His patent engine was described in detail in the *Illustrated London News* in May 1858:

'The engine is the invention of Mr. Bray of Folkestone and possesses advantages over all others in use for its simplicity and usefulness. The wheels of the traction engines adapted for ploughing or dragging weights over soft ground have not had sufficient hold upon the ground when constructed in the ordinary manner. By Bray's patented improvement the wheels are constructed with teeth or blades, which enter the ground and obtain a firm hold. The teeth are made to slide or move in and out by an eccentric motion, so that they clean themselves of the soil and are again ready to enter the ground, the smooth surface of the wheels also being cleared by means of self-acting scrapers. The eccentric is capable of adjustment, so that the projection of the teeth may be varied, and thus the wheels may at pleasure be made to act like ordinary wheels ... Experiments have been made on Broadmead Farm, Folkestone. The engine was set to work three ploughs in a frame over a light loamy soil, the ground rather wet and the quality of work done in a day of ten hours was at the rate of six acres at a cost of not more than 4s per acre,'

When Richard Garrett began manufacturing traction engines he visited America, where new techniques of mass production were being developed. He used this new idea when designing his factory, the Long Shop at Leinston, Suffolk. Parts manufactured in the side aisles and galleries were brought into the central aisle for assembly. The Long Shop is now a steam museum. The illustration comes from Meason's *Guide to the Great Eastern Railway* 1865.

The Long Shop looking East c. 1865.   (Measom's Guide to the Great Eastern Rly).

BRAY'S PATENT TRACTION-ENGINE.

William Bray was the first to use gears instead of chain drive on a traction engine. The drive wheels were fitted with blades round the circumference to provide extra traction in soft ground and the steering system was an improvement on Aveling's pilot wheel.

The farmer declared that the work had been done as well as it would have been by a team of horses. It does not seem, however, to have been a great success and the problem of adapting the traction engine to ploughing was to find a very different solution as we shall find out in the next chapter.

Bray also turned his attention to the difficult problem of steering. The front wheels were mounted on a bogey, set well in front of the boiler. The steersman stood on a platform above the front axle, which was turned by means of a horizontal wheel on a vertical shaft. By now various elements of the traction engine were beginning to come together. Many of the problems for increasing efficiency for all forms of steam locomotives had been solved on the railways before the traction engine was fully developed. In 1829, Robert Stephenson designed a locomotive to prove that it could work the planned main line between Liverpool and Manchester on a regular basis and at a reasonable speed. Up to then, boilers had been built with either a single flue or a return flue, one doubled round in a U-bend. His engine *Rocket* had a multi-tubular boiler. The firebox was jacketed to prevent heat loss, and the hot gases from the fire passed through a large number of tubes, immersed in the water in the boiler. This ensured a far greater area of hot metal was in contact with the water to produce steam. Multi-tubular boilers became standard for traction engines.

This was not the only idea borrowed from the railways. Reversing locomotives had always been a difficult operation in the early days of the steam railway. The story of how this problem was solved begins in 1841 with William Williams, a 'gentleman apprentice' – that is a young man whose wealthy parents had paid for him to learn the basics of engineering and draughtsmanship without having to go through the various grades as others would have done. He was employed at the Robert Stephenson works in Newcastle, where he began experimenting with a more efficient form of valve gear than anything else then in use. He devised a system with a slotted link, in which the gear for forward motion was coupled to the top and the eccentric for reverse to the bottom of the link. The links could be raised and lowered via the reversing lever situated on the footplate. For the first time, reversing was a smooth, continuous operation. Williams worked on his idea with a pattern maker at the works, William Howe.

There has always been some doubt as to who should be given the credit for the new system, but in the event, it was to be named after neither. It became known as the Stephenson linkage, simply because it had been produced by employees of the works and Robert Stephenson himself approved the design and put it into production. In solving one problem, the Stephenson linkage brought a new, important advantage to efficiency. Because the reversing gear was continuous, it was possible, for example, to start the

The valve gear produced at the Robert Stephenson locomotive works in Newcastle was widely adopted by traction engine manufacturers. The version shown here, with piston valves, is the version in use on many British steam locomotives, but most traction engines used slide valves instead.

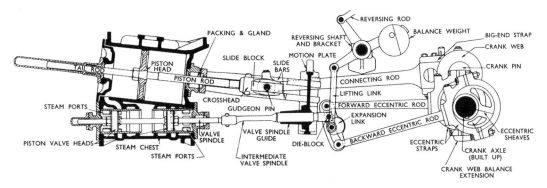

engine with the gear in the full forward position, and then ease it back towards the reverse position when the engine was moving smoothly. The effect of this was to cut off the steam inlet valve before the piston had completed its journey along the cylinder, allowing the steam to expand before it was exhausted. It is an effect not unlike putting a car into overdrive for smooth running at higher speeds. The Stephenson linkage was to be widely adopted in British traction engines.

One might have expected that with the development of the traction engine, the portable engine would become redundant, but they continued to be manufactured well into the twentieth century. Larger versions were built with compound engines. Improved boiler design and stronger materials made it possible to produce steam at ever higher pressures. Steam leaving the cylinder was still under pressure, so instead of simply being exhausted, it was passed to a second, low-pressure cylinder. In order to keep the system in balance, the low pressure cylinder had a greater diameter than the high pressure, to compensate for the fact that by the time the steam hd been used in the first cylinder it had lost some of its power.

Britain was a leader in the development of traction engines, but by no means the only country manufacturing these machines in the nineteenth century. Important manufacturers worked in both France and Germany, though often using very different designs from those favoured by British manufacturers; many had a vertical

American manufacturers, like the first British engine builders, started by producing portable engines. This drawing of an American engine with its threshing set is one of the very few nineteenth century illustrations that actually shows an engine being moved by a team of horses.

boiler with a separate chassis to provide the main frame, unlike British practice where the boiler itself was the frame. But by far the biggest manufacturers were to be found in North America. In many ways the start of the enterprise was similar to that in Britain. The story of Cooper and Co. of Mount Vernon, Ohio is typical.

The Cooper family were pioneers, moving from Pennsylvania to Knox County, Ohio in 1808. There were two sons, Charles, born in 1811 and Elias two years later. They were the founders of C & E Cooper. Although born into a farming family, the brothers decided to try their hand at other activities and began by working a small coal mine in 1832. That did not last long, and shortly afterwards they invested in the 'Old Davis' iron foundry at Mount Vernon. Their first introduction to steam power came when they installed an engine to blow air, providing the blast for the furnace. They were soon producing many different kinds of machinery, including ploughs. By the 1840s they had begun the production of conventional steam engines, fitted with the usual slide valves. These do exactly what the name suggests, slide across the openings that allow steam to enter either end of the cylinder and exhaust at the end of each stroke. In 1849, the American inventor George Corliss came up with a new idea. He had already had an interesting career. Born in New York he had started his working life in a store, but showed an aptitude for mechanical inventions. He had his first success with

In Britain, it became customary for contractors to travel from farm to farm with their engines and threshing equipment. To save money on accommodation many had 'living vans' such as this where they stayed at the end of the working day.

A contractor's threshing set fully assembled and ready to go off to start work.

a machine for stitching boots, but he soon turned his attention to steam. In 1849 he took out his first patent for a wholly new valve system. He used four valves, two steam inlets and two exhausts, situated at each end of the cylinder, and opening directly into the cylinder. He later made a further improvement, by using rotating valves instead of slide valves. It proved a very efficient system, and the Coopers decided to adopt the Corliss to make portable engines.

The first versions, which appeared around 1860, were only portable in the sense that they were small enough to be moved around. They were either pulled onto site by a team of horses or in a wagon if the ground was hard, but on soft ground they were mounted on skids. This was not very practical unless they were being taken to sites such as saw mills, where they could be used for long periods of time. But if they were intended to be used for threshing, where they had to be moved around fields on a regular basis, something else was needed. The next version, the Cooper Common Farm Engine, was mounted on wagon wheels that made it much easier to move, but it still required a team of horses to drag it around. The next step was to develop a genuine traction engine, which they did in 1875.

The system used a bevel gear and inclined shaft to transfer the drive from the crankshaft turned by the engine to the rear wheels. The gears on the wheels allowed the two wheels to be worked independently, or the gears could be disengaged from both wheels. The notion of a traction engine was completely new in America and disengaging the gearing gave cautious farmers the opportunity to continue to move the engine with horse power alone, just as the portable engines had been. Coopers need not have worried, as they themselves explained

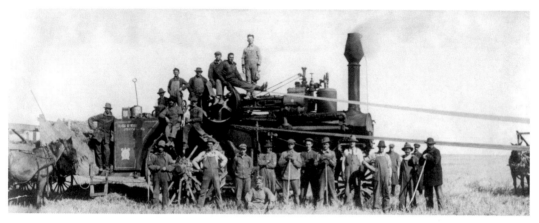

In America conditions were very different from those in Britain; with vast expanses of wheat instead of small fields. The machinery was also provided on a far greater scale, as exemplified by this Abell engine and its working crew.

in an advertisement that began with the simple statement that they were the first to build traction engines in America:

'We built our first Traction Engines in 1875, and of course at first regarded them as an experiment. They were a success, however, from the start, and greatly pleased our customers. For the first two years thereafter we gave many purchasers the option to take off and return the traction gearing at the end of the season, if it did not give satisfaction, or if actual use did not convince the owner that it was worth the extra price charged for the engine. In no case did a purchaser avail himself of this option. We first advertised the engine in our circulars for 1876, and during that year and the year 1877 we made and sold about one hundred of them. In 1878 we built Traction Engines for stock, and the result was we put out over two hundred of them that year, and yet so great was the demand that we were obliged to decline about one-third of our orders during the busy season, more than three-quarters of our farm engine orders being for Traction Engines. Our trade in 1879 and 1880 ran still stronger to Traction Engines, and although we put out about three hundred machines in 1879 and nearly four hundred in 1880 we were obliged to decline a large number of orders both seasons,'

At this stage of development, the engines still required horses to steer them, just as the British engines did. In time, a suitable form of steering would be developed and in the meantime, there was another problem to solve.

CHAPTER FOUR

Ploughing by Steam

The earliest reference to ploughing by steam seems to date from 1812 when Richard Trevithick placed an advert offering portable engines, weighing 15 hundredweight, suitable for threshing, grinding and sawing at a price of £63 and a heavier engine for ploughing at £105. He also worked at developing an entirely new form of ploughing engine. As he wrote in a letter to Sir Charles Sinclair in 1812, 'It is my opinion that every part of agriculture might be performed by steam.' He designed a machine that could be used for cultivating common land; it was first to be used to loosen the soil, and then the revolving spades were adapted to throw the soil to one side, creating a pattern of ridge and furrow. He sent a drawing to the Rastrick foundry at Bridgnorth for this engine and suggested that it could be worked using a locomotive similar to the ones already tried successfully on rails, and he made the point that as the wheels did not slip on iron rails, they would hold firmly to the ground and provide sufficient traction. What we do not know is whether or not the machine was ever properly tested, let alone went into production. The drawings show only the mechanism, not the boiler that was being made in Cornwall. One thing is clear, that as it is shown with a shaft at the front, it was to be towed, not self-propelling. He did, however, suggest that it could be used with a form of locomotive, similar to the one he had already built and demonstrated on the Penydarren tramway in South Wales. Rastrick was dubious, but Trevithick reassured him:

> 'There is no doubt about the wheels turning around as you suppose, for when that engine in Wales travelled on the tramroad, which was very smooth, yet all the power of the engine could not slip around the wheels when the engine was chained to a post for that particular experiment.'

Trevithick's machine never went into production and had no immediate successor, but in 1847 the Frenchman Pierre Barrat produced an even more elaborate version of the cultivator.

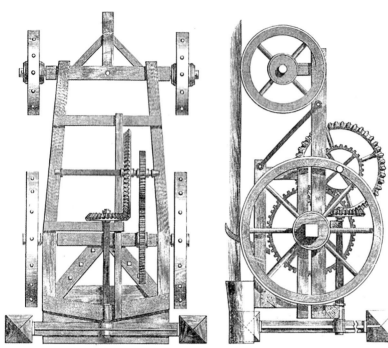

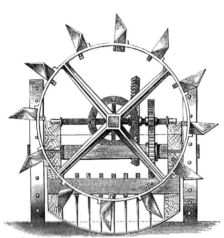

One of the earliest attempts to plough using steam power was made by Richard Trevithick. This is his 'plough' as sketched by his son Francis from his father's original drawings, though it is rather like a modern rotavator. It was never in fact put into production, though Trevithick envisaged it working in conjunction with some form of steam tractor.

Instead of square-bladed spades it had pointed mattocks that were designed to both dig into the soil and twist. It seems never to have gone into production either. A far more practical scheme was dreamed up across the Atlantic in 1833 by Edmund C. Bellinger of South Carolina. He drew up plans for a system in which the plough would be hauled over the ground by cable which, as we shall see shortly, would be successfully developed in Britain, but for some reason Bellinger's system never went into production.

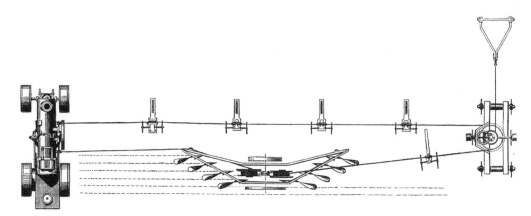

John Fowler produced the first successful steam ploughing system. In its original form, shown in this diagram, the plough was pulled across the field by means of a cable from a drum under the engine to a pulley on the far side of the field, with smaller pulleys to support the cable on its return to the engine. The large pulley was mounted on a carriage, so that it could be moved along once a furrow was completed.

There were several attempts to come up with working systems in various parts of the world, but none was entirely satisfactory. Yet it was very obvious that a system would be of huge value in raising productivity, particularly in Britain with its rapidly growing, and increasingly urbanised population. In 1854 the Royal Agricultural Society of England (RASE) offered a prize of £200, roughly £12,000 at today's prices, 'for a steam cultivator that shall, in the most efficient manner, turn over the soil and be an economic substitute for the plough or the spade.' A winner would not only receive this quite substantial sum, but would be able to go into production with the backing and the approval of a prestigious organisation. Contests were held in 1855, 1856 and 1857, but without the prize being awarded, though a special medal was presented to one of the entrants for his efforts. This was John Fowler, who had worked for a number of years at devising mechanical means of improving the land.

Fowler was born at Melksham in Wiltshire in 1826, where his father was a merchant and a leading member of the Quaker community. John seemed set to follow in his father's footsteps, beginning his working life as a corn merchant but soon turned away to follow his true vocation, joining the engineering firm of Wilson and Gilkes of Middlesbrough in 1847. Shortly afterwards he visited Ireland, then in the grip of the terrible potato famine. One of the problems that he saw was that too much of the land was useless for growing crops because of poor drainage – and the cost of drainage was too high to make projects viable. Back in England in 1850, he set about looking at ways of mechanising the process in partnership with Albert Fry of Bristol. Fry had recently acquired a coach building works – he was one of the few members of the family who did not get involved in making chocolate. Together they began work on building a drainage plough

He did not look at steam power in the first instance. The mole that dug the trench to hold the drainage pipes was dragged across the field by means of a capstan worked by horses. His next version was an improvement. In this system, the horses drove a vertical winch, from which a rope stretched along the edge of the field to a fixed pulley, and then was passed at right angles to the mole on the far side of the field. As the mole was dragged along, pipes were automatically dropped into the ditch behind it. The next step was very obvious. Instead of using a horse to turn the winch, he mounted it on the front of a portable steam engine. He then realised that exactly the same system could be adapted for use with a plough instead of a mole digging a ditch.

There was still a problem to be overcome. When ploughing with a team of horses, it is a simple matter to turn the team and their plough at the headland for the return journey. but this proved more troublesome with the steam plough. He solved this difficulty by designing a new type of plough. This version had two sets of ploughshares, fitted at either end of the frame. These were pivoted, so that when one set was embedded in the ground, turning over the soil, the other set was stuck up in the air. So instead of having to turn the whole thing round at the end of a run, it was only necessary to drop one set down and raise the other. The only adjustment necessary was to move the anchored pulley along by the width of one furrow for the next pass.

The new plough was built by Ransome and exhibited at the R.A.S.E. meeting of 1856 and again in 1857. By this time, the prize money had been increased to £500 but it was still not awarded, although in the same year the Royal Highland and Agricultural Society of Scotland did give him a £200 award. And when Fowler made yet another attempt at the R.A.S.E. competition at Salisbury in 1858, he finally got his award. He had actually patented a different version that did away with the pulley system and used a pair of engines, with cable drums to pull the plough from one to the other. He continued to favour the single engine system on the grounds of cost, but in time it was the double engine system that became the accepted method for steam ploughing. Fowler had been worried about the cost to the average farmer of having to buy two engines, but in practice steam ploughs were rarely used by individuals. As with the threshing sets, specialist teams moved from farm to farm throughout the ploughing season.

The ploughs were a huge success, with a hundred sets at work by 1860. Manufacture moved several times, first to the Robert Stephenson works at Newcastle, then in 1860 to Kitson & Hewitson of Hunslet, Leeds. A new Steam Plough Works was established next to the Hunslet site, and by 1863 it was simply John Fowler & Co. The works now employed some 400 men and Fowler was constantly thinking up new inventions and took out 32 patents, not just for agricultural machinery but for such diverse subjects as steam engine slide valves and machines for making bricks and tiles. All this hard work affected his health, and in 1864 he retired and was advised to take on a more active life. He decided on hunting, but in a fall from his horse he fractured his arm, was infected by tetanus and died in December of that year. But by then Fowler engines were at work all over central Europe and as far away as the cotton fields of Egypt. The biggest engines could carry as much as 1800 feet (550m) of heavy metal cable. The movement of the cable was determined by the only difference in the two engines, one being built for the cable to emerge to the right of the engine, the other to the left. In both cases, the cable was passed through a pulley system at the end of a short arm, known as a 'monkey's head' – though the derivation of the name is not immediately obvious, as there is nothing very ape-like in its appearance. The drums themselves were activated by means of gearing from the crankshaft, engaged by a lever working on a dog clutch. The speed of the drums was kept constant by means of a friction band. The ploughing engines were generally bigger and heavier then ordinary traction engines, to avoid them being pulled over by the power of the cable; they also had greater boiler capacity to reduce the number of times they needed to be topped up during the working days.

In Britain, one of the biggest contractors was Ward and Duke of Sleaford in Lincolnshire, who in 1908 owned 24 pairs of engines with their ploughs and cultivation machinery. Their engines were all compounds, with the usual arrangement of high pressure and low pressure cylinders. In 1914, the company was responsible for ploughing almost 65,000 acres of land in an area stretching from Lincolnshire as far as Northamptonshire. They worked with crews

An essential part of the Fowler system was the plough itself. As it was required to go backwards and forwards across a field, but could not be turned round, it was double-headed. As seen here, one set of ploughshares is at work, while the other sticking up in the sir, will be lowered for the return journey and the next furrow.

of five, two men to drive the engines, one man to steer the plough, a boy to act as cook and general dogsbody. They worked from dawn to dusk, with very little in the way of breaks. The boy would prepare simple food, such as boiled bacon and potato, and the men would eat one at a time, the foreman taking over from the one who was taking his break. That way, the work never had to stop. The work was not necessarily as physically tiring as manual labour, but required great concentration at all times, to ensure that the engines were accurately positioned and furrows straight.

Some contractors combined ploughing work with threshing, and work for the threshing crews was no less demanding and the crews worked equally long hours. The contractor would often have a whole series of machines to assemble. He might have the threshing drum itself, a trussing machine that would make the straw into bales and perhaps an elevator to lift them for loading. Some outfits also included a chaff cutter to cut up the leftover material into low quality winter feed. Then once the team had been assembled, the engine oiled and fuelled, the tender filled and the water tank topped up, it was all ready to move out to the next farm. The roads of nineteenth century Britain were by no means all of the highest quality and those of rural areas were generally the worst; many farms could only be reached down narrow, winding lanes. But these difficulties were compounded in the 1860s by government legislation – the Locomotive Acts. The first Act of 1861 was generally a reasonable affair, with rules such as having a crew of at least two on an engine, which would normally be the case anyway,

Savory's System of Steam Cultivation.

Fowler improved his system by using two engines, each with a cable drum under the body, so that the plough could be hauled along between them. At the end of a furrow, each engine would move forward by the same amount for the next stage. This system remained in general use in Britain for many years.

and extra men where other vehicles were being towed. A speed limit of 10mph in the country and 5mph in built-up areas was also acceptable. But four years later Parliament introduced far more stringent rules. Speeds were now reduced to 4mph in the country and 2mph in towns and villages. Engines had to have a crew of three, though what the third was supposed to do was far from clear. And, most famously – or infamously – if two or more vehicles were attached a man had to walk 60 paces in front of the engine with a red flag so as to be able to assist horse-drawn vehicles to pass the train. It was thanks to this last rule that the legislation became universally known as the Red Flag Act. It certainly did nothing to make life easier for those trying to move their agricultural teams around the country. Ostensibly the laws had been passed to prevent heavy, self-propelling engines from damaging the roads; many thought with some justification that the rules were made to pacify conservative country squires and to appease the vociferous lobbying by those who worked with all forms of horse transport.

Once the team arrived at the farm, the engine was brought to the first stack to be threshed. The drum had to be levelled up with jacks and chocks, then the engine run round to a point just far enough away for the belt from the flywheel to the pulley on the threshing machine to be at the right tension. This was a job requiring a lot of experience and a good eye. Then work could begin. The thatch that had protected the stack from the weather was removed and the machinery started up. One man would be on the stack, throwing the sheaths down to the feeder, who cut the binding twine and carefully spread the grain and lowered it down the concave shield.

As the day wore on, the air became thick with dust and the work got harder. It was fairly easy tossing sheathes from the top of the stack, but as the stack lowered, the man had to start pitchforking it up.to the top of the drum. The stacks were usually home to previously contented and undisturbed inhabitants; rats and mice found such places not only very snug but they also came with a built-in larder. Now they were dispossessed, and they scuttled off for safety; one reason the workers tied string round the lower parts of their trousers was that the rodents considered trouser legs as likely refuges. Terriers were often kept next to the work, and had a merry time pursuing the escapees. The men on the team had no time to watch the spectacle of rat chasing, for their lives were extraordinarily busy with long hours of often arduous work. The season was short and it was imperative to make use of every hour of daylight to make as much money as possible before harvest time came to an end.

There was no question of anyone expecting to go home at the end of a day's work, and lodging was often hard to find. Landladies were, it seems, unwilling to accept sooty, grimy men into their pristine homes. Fowler introduced 'living vans', which were little better than wooden shacks on wheels, fitted with rudimentary bunk beds – and a little desk for the foreman to complete his paperwork for the day. If the men were lucky, there might be enough time to visit the local pub to help wash down the accumulated dust of the day, but late nights were definitely out. The morning start ensured that.

Threshing would normally start around 7 a.m., but the engine men were at work long before that. The firebox had to be cleared out and a fire lit, and the temperature gradually increased as steam pressure slowly climbed towards working pressure. There would be a short break for breakfast, and then perhaps half an hour for lunch, eaten out in the fields. When threshing finished, usually between five and six in the afternoon, clinker and ashes had to be removed and the engine sheeted up ready for work the next day. By the time everything was sorted out, the team would have been busy for well over twelve hours. Whether the work involved threshing or ploughing, the outfits themselves were generally owned by contractors who could afford the high purchase price. It was seasonal and the workers were generally laid off once the ploughing season came to an end, finding whatever work they could until they were hired again the following year. It was a hard life, but the contractors played an important role in the life of the countryside. Ward and Duke may have been the biggest but they were by no means the only contractors, providing a full range of steam-powered agricultural services to farmers all over Britain.

Steam ploughing in North America developed on very different lines from that of Britain. The late nineteenth century saw the opening of the American mid-west and the Prairie Provinces of Canada. This was not a question of working within an existing field system, established over generations, but of breaking new ground and creating vast fields for growing grain. The British system, using cable, never really caught on across the Atlantic. Instead, they used increasingly powerful machines to pull ploughs, with large numbers of ploughshares or 'bottoms'. Because of the often harsh conditions on the windswept prairies, many engines were built with canopies and the Russell engines offered the ultimate in luxury with enclosed cabs fitted with sliding windows. The Americans prided themselves on producing the best engines in the world – and individual manufacturers assumed that theirs were simply the best of the best, as this catalogue entry for Port Huron engines makes clear:

> 'There are three classes of traction engine.
> 'Heavy Weight, as English makes – Built much heavier in some parts than necessary for the work they have to do.
> 'Middle Weight – Port Huron, correctly proportioned. Each part designed especially for the work it has to do and the strain it has to stand.
> 'Light Weight – Those American and Canadian makes built with the sole idea of making them light weight without regard to correct proportions.'

Nichols and Shepard took a rather more direct approach, with their simple message:

> 'If you don't buy your engine off us, you don't buy your engine right.'

As the years went by and technology improved, especially with the wider availability of good quality steel, engines became ever bigger and more powerful, and a number of manufacturers built compound engines. The Advance Threshing Company claimed that their compounds, working at a boiler pressure of 150psi, were 28 per cent more efficient than their simple engines working at 120psi. But few could match the American Abell for sheer size and power. The company was founded by John Abell, who was born in England in 1822, emigrated to Canada and settled near Toronto in 1845. He worked for a couple of years for a firm of coach builders, before he set up his own manufacturing business, the first in the region to have machine tools powered by steam. He began making farming equipment, including his own design of a threshing engine. In 1874 his premises burned down, but the disaster brought the opportunity for a fresh start and he began manufacturing portable engines, later developing them into traction engines, worked by friction belts.

In 1897, when British forces were at war in India, a young Scots soldier was awarded the Victoria Cross. Although seriously injured,

Steam ploughing being demonstrated at the Great Dorset Steam Fair. The cable can be clearly seen stretching away to the second engine.

A large American ploughing engine photographed in 1895. There are a number of differences between this and the British steam plough. Here the engine is simply acting as a tractor, pulling a conventional plough. The fringed canopy protecting the driver was necessary given the very different climate conditions, and like most American engines this was built to be fired with wood not coal, so has a bulbous spark-arresting chimney.

he continued playing 'Cock O' The North' on his bagpipes to encourage his comrades. The story made the young man famous and Abell promptly adopted the name of the tune for his engines, and used a rooster as his emblem. Unmarried and with no heirs, Abell sold the business when he reached the age of eighty and it became the American Abell Company. The engines were still known as 'Cock O' The North' and the mightiest of these were used for ploughing the prairies. One of these engines began its working life in Saskatchewan in 1913 and was a real monster of a machine, weighing in at 44,000lb. It regularly pulled a 12-bottom plough, consumed 5,000lb of coal a day and in that time could turn over four acres of prairie. It required a crew of twenty-two and they kept a couple of cooks busy providing them with food. This splendid engine is now in the care of the Western Development Museum in Saskatchewan.

In Britain, Fowler's continued to make improvements in their ploughing systems, introducing the anti-balance plough. The balanced version, was easy to manipulate, switching from one set of shares to the other. But it had the disadvantage that the working end could lift out of the furrow. In the anti-balance, when the tension came on the cable, the wheels moved forward, altering the point of balance, so that the working end remained firmly in the ground. Even so, it was not the perfect answer to cultivation. When working in fields with a dense coverage of weeds, the stubble and other matter were not always completely buried when the sods were turned. The answer was the steam cultivator, usually in the form of rotating blades that dug and turned the ground, not unlike the device designed by Trevithick many years earlier. The commonest variety, known as 'grubbers' came in a variety of sizes, with the largest having eleven tines and capable of working up to forty acres of land in a day. Most fields were cultivated using the 'done and crossed' system, in which after working the field in one direction, it would then be worked again at right angles to the first.

Fowler's were always at the forefront of innovation, even after the death of their founder in 1864. By the late nineteenth century, the Steam Plough Works was employing some 600 workers and turning out machines at the rate of one a week. The arrangement of the winding drum was altered with the introduction of the horizontal shaft engines. The name comes from the arrangement by which the drum was turned by a shaft meshing with the crankshaft through bevel gearing. Engines were being made in a variety of different sizes, specified by an initial letter; the B4s for example were 8 horse power and the Z 14 horse power. The change from ploughs to cultivators required a new modification. The cultivator had to be pulled across the field at a faster rate than the modest 4mph of the plough, so a new class of engine, the BB, was introduced that doubled the rope speed to pull the cultivator at 8mph. Many of the surviving engines are of this class and, although they are normally now described as ploughing engines, they could more accurately be called cultivator engines.

Fowler's were, of course, not the only company producing ploughing engines and though most were built on the Fowler pattern, some went their own way. J & F Howard of Bedford, for example, produced an engine with a transverse boiler and an enormous winding drum set behind it. Other companies built engines with vertical drums that fed the cable out through a pulley. Howard's 'Farmer's Friend' had a detachable drum, so that it could be converted for use with a threshing drum.

Ploughing engines could be used for both ploughing and cultivating, and could also be adapted for harrowing and rolling. They were also used in dredging lakes and reservoirs, where a heavy bucket was hauled across the bottom of the lake. The ploughing engine was a versatile machine and Fowler's were able to offer systems to suit all kinds of situations and different types of ground, offering a staggering seven hundred variations on their standard plough. The steam plough and the traction engine both played vital roles in the modernisation of agriculture in the nineteenth century. Steam power was also to play an equally important part in improving road transport.

CHAPTER FIVE

The Steam Roller

It is generally agreed that in most of Europe at the beginning of the eighteenth century roads were in a poorer condition than they had been during the days of the Roman Empire. The first successful attempts to produce a better system came in France where the Corps des Ponts et Chaussées – Corps of Bridges and Roads – was established in 1716. It was not immediately effective, but in 1747 a school for training civil engineers was established that supplied professionals for the Corps. By 1776, France had rationalised their whole highway system. Roads were graded from the first class, those leading from Paris to other major cities, that had to be 42 metres wide between the boundary fences, down to the fourth class, connecting small towns and villages that only had to be 24 metres wide. A system developed for laying roads that began with digging a trench in which large stones were laid as a foundation, on top of which smaller stones were spread and rammed down hard after which a third layer of even smaller stones were added. The system was improved by Pierre Trésaguet, who made a firmer foundation by laying the stones on edge, which were then beaten into place by hand using hammers; then, as before, two layers of decreasingly sized stones were placed on top and also beaten into place. He insisted that only the hardest stones should be used for the top surface, even if they had to be brought from distant quarries, to ensure durability.

Before the eighteenth century in Britain, little attempt was made to improve roads. Instead various laws were passed in an attempt to ensure that heavy vehicles were fitted with broad wheels that would not dig into the surface to make deep ruts. The legislation was mostly a dismal failure. Among the first attempts to build a better, more durable system was brought about by military, not civil, needs. Following the Jacobite uprisings in Scotland, it became very obvious that the army needed better roads to try to keep control of the Highlands and a system was set up under General Wade, which produced roads with a durable stone surface. In England, pioneers such as 'Blind Jack' Metcalf of Knaresborough in Yorkshire set about surveying new roads in the

Aveling and Porter's pioneering steam roller being demonstrated in Hyde Park, London in 1864. Essentially it was one of their standard traction engines but with the wheels made considerably wider to act as rollers. The gap between the wheels is the same width as the rollers, so that the engine can then roll the strip in the centre with accuracy by moving just one wheel's width to the side.

latter part of the eighteenth century. A system, very similar to that used by Trésaguet, was developed in Britain by Thomas Telford and used in building the Holyhead Road. But both the Trésaguet and Telford systems used a great deal of material and were very expensive to construct. A cheaper system was developed by the Scots engineer John McAdam.

McAdam was born in Scotland in 1756 but emigrated to New York, where he became a successful business man. He returned to Scotland in 1783 and was appointed as one of the Road Trustees for Ayrshire, where he spent a great deal of his own money on road repairs and trying out different construction methods, By 1815 he felt he had the answer to the best system to use and built some 180 miles of roads for the Bristol Road Trusts using his new method. The main difference was that he no longer relied on a foundation layer of massive stones, as he explained very clearly:

'That it is the native soil which really supports the weight of traffic; that while it is preserved in a dry state, it will carry any weight without sinking and that it does in fact carry the road and carriages also; that this native soil must be previously made quite dry and a covering impenetrable to rain must then be placed over it in that dry state; that the thickness of the road should only be regulated by the quantity of material necessary to form such impervious covering and never by any reference to its own power of carrying weight.'

A McAdam road was built up of successive layers of small stones – he insisted on using a two-inch diameter ring as a check and decreed that no stone should weigh more than six ounces. Generally, the stones were laid in three stages, being compacted as each level was added.

These various systems all depended on compacting the layers of stone with rollers. The first cast iron rollers, pulled by horses, were introduced in France in 1787. These had cylinders that were 8ft wide and 3ft in diameter and weighed roughly 3½ tons. The idea was not immediately taken up, as many engineers felt that the damage done by the horses' hooves outweighed any advantages provided by the heavy roller. Such rollers were only introduced into Britain in 1815 for compacting McAdam-type roads. However, the arrival of the steam railway brought about a change in attitude. Roads were now considered of less importance and many were allowed to deteriorate. Repairs consisted of little more than spreading stones over damaged surfaces and relying on the traffic to compact and flatten them. But it soon became obvious that railways had their limitations and good roads were still absolutely essential. It was time to get out the rollers again. The objection to using horses was sensible, and there was an obvious alternative – do away with the horses and power the rollers by steam.

The first experiments with steam were once again made in France. Two versions were produced, one in 1859 by Lemoine and the other by Ballaison in 1861. Not much is known about either inventor, but the two engines were put to the test and the trials widely reported. This account appeared in the *Daily Times* of New Zealand in August 1866, quoting London's *Pall-Mall Gazette*:

'A series of experiments has been carried out for some time past by the municipality of Paris in order to test the comparative merits of the Lemoine and Ballaison steam locomotives employed in crushing and consolidating the broken granite laid on the streets of that city. It has at last been decided that the Ballaison locomotive is the better of the two. It has two rollers, the engine being between them, and the boiler on one of them. The motion is communicated by a chain. With fuel and water, the weight of the Ballaison is 13½ tons with springs and an iron frame weighs 15½ tons. Its force is 6 horse-power and its consumption of coal about 16lb per hour. It does its work in half the time and at half the cost that would be required were the work done by horses, and the work is done more rapidly and completely. It may now be seen at all hours of the day crushing smooth the granite of the new boulevards of Paris and in the more crowded thoroughfares it works only at night.'

The Ballaison roller was manufactured by Gellerat et Cie of Paris, in two versions of 8½ and 15 tons.

Although Britain was a pioneer of traction engines, they were not among the first to develop rollers, mainly because of the system that had developed for road construction. The McAdam road was a success, but in Britain the maintenance of roads fell foul of the system under which they were built and controlled. In some cases, the maintenance was down to local parish councils, who could call on local citizens for repair work. As this was unpaid there was no incentive to do a workmanlike job; most repairs consisted of little more than throwing some stones into the larger potholes. The main roads between cities and major towns were nearly all turnpikes, administered by Trusts who paid for their construction and then charged tolls for their use. In theory the tolls were intended to pay for maintenance, but some Trusts were far more concerned with their own profits. Some were notoriously bad. The noted agriculturist Arthur Young who spent a great deal of time travelling around the country in the late eighteenth century had this to say about the Wigan turnpike:

'I know not in the whole range of language, terms sufficiently expressive to describe this infernal road.

'Let me most seriously caution all travellers, who may accidentally purpose to travel this terrible country, to avoid it as they would the devil; for a thousand to one but they break their necks or their limbs by overthrows or breaking downs. They will here meet with ruts which I actually measured four feet deep, and floating with mud only from a wet summer; what therefore must it be in winter?'

Some Trusts not only neglected essential maintenance but also proved unscrupulous in their profiteering. In South Wales, they erected more and more gates to increase revenue and the costs to those using the roads. This resulted in a wave of rioting, in which gates were demolished and toll houses destroyed. They became known as the 'Rebecca Riots' from a Biblical quote that the descendants of Rebecca would hold the gate of her enemies and the rioters, calling themselves Rebecca and Her Children, dressed as women to disguise their identity. The result was a Parliamentary enquiry that led to the passing of several Acts that took away much of the power of the Trusts and made it law to maintain the highways. There was finally an incentive for improvement.

William Bray built what was described at the time as a steam roller, but it was simply a common road roller, pulled by a traction

When Aveling started to build more conventional machines with a single, wide roller at the front, they needed to devise a new steering mechanism. The device they came up with is seen here, with the chains leading to either side of the front roller and controlled by a conventional steering wheel.

The steam rollers produced by Buffalo-Springfield in America were very different from their British counterparts. This 1924 Blue Buffalo has the typical 'coffee pot' vertical boiler of these engines.

engine instead of horses. The first British innovation occurred not at home, but across the sea in Imperial India. W.E. Batho was a Birmingham engineer working in Calcutta and he designed a steam roller in conjunction with the chief engineer of the city, W. Clark, in 1863. Batho was later to return to Britain, where he was to play an important role in developing the road roller working with the man who was to be responsible for the basic design of roller that persisted in Britain into the twentieth century, Thomas Aveling.

Aveling had developed a successful business in constructing traction engines and there is some doubt as to why he decided to turn to steam rollers. As is so often the case, a legend has developed surrounding his decision, which may or no may not be true, but certainly makes sense. In this story, he was strolling through his home town of Rochester, when he saw a group of labourers struggling to haul along a crude roller, consisting of an iron cylinder packed with cement, in order to crush the surface stones on a new road. The man who had famously commented on the absurdity of seeing a steam engine pulled by horses, found this sight equally ridiculous. Here was, he thought, an obvious case where steam power was better than man power. His first efforts in 1865, like Bray's, simply involved using a traction engine to haul an improvised heavy roller – it had started life as a cast iron section of a pier. When he looked at the result he realised that the heavy wheels of the engine itself had done a better job of crushing the stone than the roller. The next step was to transform the traction engine, so that it could do the job even more efficiently.

His first machine was based on the existing twelve horse power traction engine. He increased the diameter of the two rear wheels by a metre, and doubled the width – in effect turning them into a pair of rollers. As they moved along, they rolled two strips, leaving an unrolled section in the centre. This was necessary, as the engine was still being steered by a pilot wheel at the front. To treat the complete surface, the roller had to be moved along by one roll width to cover the untreated central section. He realised that this was not very satisfactory as the pilot wheel was inclined to cut a groove in the surface that was not flattened out by subsequent rolling. He set about designing a new steering system. In the redesigned roller, there was now a single wide, front wheel, mounted within an iron frame. Chains from each side of the frame were attached to a pulley system beneath the engine that could be operated by means of a steering wheel. Depending on the direction in which the wheel was turned, the chain either pulled the frame and the front roller to the left or the right. Such a system was not new, having been in use for some time in ships, where the wheel and chain were used to move the rudder. It became usual practice with steam rollers to divide the front wheel, so that in effect it consisted of a pair of cylinders. They moved independently on the axle, which made cornering a good deal easier. It is still quite tricky steering a steam roller. It takes a little time to take up the slack on the chain, so the steerer has to anticipate the action and begin turning the wheel slightly before the engine actually needs to make the movement. The system, however, was so successful that it was soon adopted for all forms of traction engine.

The steam roller arrived at just the right time, as several things were happening in road construction that were to make it increasingly valuable. For a start, new road surfaces were being developed. In 1858, a stretch of Oxford Street in London had been reset with wooden blocks. In order to prevent them getting wet in rainy weather and swelling to create an uneven surface, they were covered with a top dressing of hot pitch. Originally this was done by the crude method of dipping large watering cans with coarse roses into the portable tar boiler. The system was improved by having the horse-drawn tar boiler fitted with a sprinkler, so that it left an even layer of tar behind it as it moved along. The next stage was to use the same technique to provide a covering for MacAdam surfaces – not only keeping them watertight, but keeping down the dust that inevitably arose as the surface of small stones wore down. It was then discovered that an even better result could be obtained by mixing the top layer of road metal with the tar and

Not all American rollers were built on the Buffalo-Springfield model. This road gang is at work in Westfield, Mass. but could just as easily be at work on a British road. The photograph appeared in *Popular Science Monthly*.

laying it down to a thickness of from four to six inches. The result was the tarmacadam or more familiarly tarmac road. Producing the smooth surface from the soft material, before it had a chance to harden, was exactly the sort of job for which the steam roller was perfectly suited.

Making new roads is an expensive business, and before authorities did anything they had to be faced with serious demands for change – and there was a general feeling that thanks to the development of railways, roads were no longer a priority. But there was a group who were demanding smoother and better surfaces and those demands grew more and more vociferous as a new form of transport became increasingly popular; the bicycle. The first machines were developed in France, but by 1865 British cycling manufacture had become established in Coventry. Bicycles were not cheap, but that meant that those who did buy them were respectable citizens and, more importantly as far as authorities were concerned, citizens who had the vote. The late nineteenth century saw the steady spread of macadamised roads and an increasing demand for the services of steam rollers.

On 1 December 1866, the Commissioner for Works contracted for Avening's new roller to be put to work in Hyde Park. London for a trial period. There were favourable comments in the press at the time and in March 1867, the leading technical journal of the day, *The Engineer*, announced that Aveling had received an order for a 22-ton roller from Liverpool. 'It is to be the same as that now working in Hyde Park, viz. a 12-horse engine with its driving wheels weighted, each to be between five and six tons. Nearly twenty applications have been made to the same makers from other corporations relative to the supply of similar engines.' What came to be known as the Liverpool engines were to form the basis for later development. The Liverpoool City Surveyor reported himself well pleased with the work that cost a modest £1 a day and produced a smooth surface that was not only durable but easily cleaned. The other applications also came from the increasingly populous industrial towns and cities of the north, such as Leeds, Sheffield and Manchester – places that were already exhibiting their civic pride in their vast and elaborately decorated town halls. But there were also enquiries from one London borough, Islington and, nearer to Aveling's home base, from Maidstone in Kent.

The Liverpool engine was actually something of an anomaly, in that the overall arrangement was the reverse of what one would expect. Although this was the first time that the two front wheels had been brought together to create a single roller, they were no longer used for steering; the steering mechanism was applied to the rear wheels. This must have been extraordinarily difficult to control. The drive was applied to the front wheels. Aveling must very soon have realised that this was far from perfect and the next generation of rollers all had the more familiar configuration: steering by front wheels, power to rear wheels.

Aveling went on to make a number of improvements. All the working parts of the engine were bolted directly onto the boiler, which, with the heavy work load, caused strains in the metalwork that in turn extended the bolt holes allowing steam to escape and allowing corrosion round the edges. Aveling solved this problem by extending the sides of the firebox upwards to create 'hornplates' to which the working parts could be securely fastened. He also looked at another problem, the tendency of the engines to skid. He redesigned the arrangement of wheels and roller, with the roller now at the front, consisting of conical split rollers and conventional front wheel steering. These were an instant success and order books were soon full. Aveling had adopted a horse rearing up on its hind legs and soon the Kentish horse was prancing around the world. They proved to be wonderfully sturdy and reliable machines. One roller was ordered by the road department in Oslo in 1878. In 1918 a new driver took over and continued in the job right up to his retirement in 1960. The city authority were quite happy to let the old engine continue working but could not find anyone willing to drive it. After such a long and honourable career, however, it was not going to be sent to the scrap heap. The driver Trygve Stromberg came out of retirement to drive his engine for the very last time, as it set off garlanded with flowers and accompanied by a brass band for its final journey to a place of honour in the Oslo Museum of Science and Technology.

The first steam rollers to be used in America were supplied by Aveling, a company which over the years was to appear as Aveling and Porter and later Aveling and Barford. They were to be used in Brooklyn and Central Park, New York in 1869. The engine that went to Brooklyn was set to work in the 585-acre Prospect Park. It trundled along day and night for two months and at the end of the trial the engineer in charge wrote a glowing report. 'One day's rolling at a cost of ten dollars, gives the same result as two days rolling with the old seven ton roller, pulled by eight horses at a cost of forty dollars.'

Inevitably the Americans soon began to construct steam rollers of their own – generally referred to as steam road rollers. As in Britain, the major manufacturing firms grew out of a background of making agricultural machinery. The brothers John and Hiram Pitts initially followed their father's trade as blacksmiths, but both were interested in machinery and in 1830 they developed a new type of threshing machine. By 1837, they had gone into production in a modest way at the Pitts Agricultural Works. Their business grew rapidly and soon changed it name to Buffalo Pitts and after the brothers had retired would begin to manufacture portable engines and traction engines. The move to steam rollers did not happen until 1902, when a separate Steam Roller Works was established in Buffalo, New York. Like the larger, original works, the new factory was equipped with all the latest machinery and was among the

A beautifully preserved Marshall steam roller being given an outing by its owners, the Hurley family. Built in 1926, it remained in use with Leicestershire County Council right through to 1960.

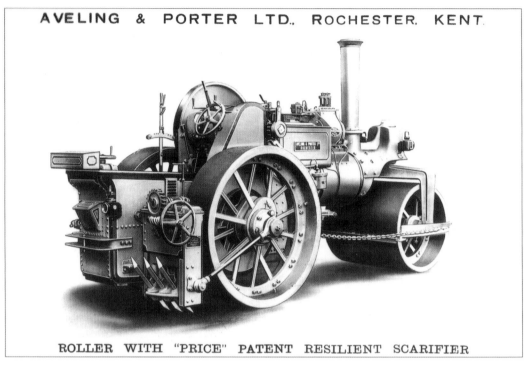

AVELING & PORTER LTD., ROCHESTER. KENT.

ROLLER WITH "PRICE" PATENT RESILIENT SCARIFIER

An Aveling and Porter roller fitted with a scarifier. This is the toothed piece of equipment behind the rear wheel that was used to break up an old road surface to form a foundation when new tarmac was laid.

first to have them powered by electricity, following the opening of the pioneering hydroelectric plant at Niagara Falls in 1899. The company later merged with the Springfield Road Roller Co. to form Buffalo-Springfield. They were to become one of the leading manufacturers of road rollers in America.

When they first began making steam rollers at the Buffalo works, they were all of very conventional design, but with Buffalo-Springfield there were some radical changes, notably the introduction of vertical boilers. There were other innovations being developed by different manufacturers in various countries. One problem that needed to be dealt with was the need to roll the hot material quickly while it was still soft. Aveling & Porter introduced their tandem rollers in 1902 that could work equally successfully in either direction. There was still something of problem, as early engines had to close off the steam valve before engaging the reversing gear. One solution to this was the 'coffee pot' rollers, such as those produced by Buffalo-Springfield, where the vertical boiler fed two identical cylinders that could be worked independently, one for forward motion the other for reverse. There was no flywheel, and a new type of eccentric gear, the King gear, made the change from one cylinder to the other almost instantaneous.

The war years of 1914-18 necessarily saw British factories turning from their normal products to the machines of war. After the war Aveling became initially concerned with improving their production methods. The Rochester factory still relied on the old technique of bringing parts to the engine as they were needed, so that it was built up on the spot. By now, the mass production techniques associated with the Ford factory in America were generally accepted as being far superior, and Aveling began the move towards mass production. These were not the only changes that came in during the post-war years. The most important was the change from slide valves to piston valves, once again following the trend set by railway locomotive engineers. The valves had two advantages: they were more efficient and cheaper to make. They did present occasional problems. On steep hills, if the boiler was full, there was the possibility of water getting into the valve. When this happened with slide valves it could leak out, but with the piston valve it simply

Robey produced a variation on the standard roller design. This is a tandem roller, with equally sized single rollers at front and back.

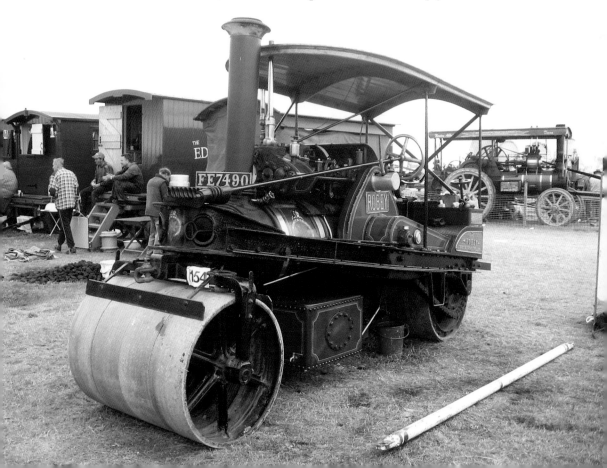

blew off the cover. A safety measure was introduced in the form of a spring-loaded escape valve. Aveling also began offering customers a much wider choice of rollers: they could order single or compound engines, front roller or tandem roller and various sizes ranging from six to twenty tons.

William Barford of the Queen Street Engineering Works of Peterborough began making rollers and was soon joined by a new partner, Thomas Perkins. Barford and Perkins rollers were not intended as road rollers, but as heavy rollers for parks, gardens and sports fields. Their flirtation with steam, however, was comparatively brief, and they continued to make heavy rollers. There was, however, sufficient overlap between them and more conventional steam roller manufacturers to go into partnership and a new company Aveling and Porter was formed, but only just in time for the end of steam. What was assumed would be the last steam roller trundled out of the Rochester works in 1947, but in 1950 they received what was to be the real final farewell to steam when Armstrong Vickers put in an order for rollers for Thailand and Indonesia. It was not, of course, the end of the business; Barford had started making diesel powered rollers as early as 1904.

A typical British road gang, probably photographed in the 1930s. Although the steam roller was vital, most of the heavy work was still down to the work gang with their hand tools.

Individual manufacturers introduced variations from the more standard designs. Wallis & Stevens introduced differential gears, but most rollers simply had a very low gear, appropriate for engines designed to spend most of their working lives at a slow walking pace. Burrell's had been among the pioneers of single-crank compound engines and they adapted these as road rollers. They proved very successful and had a healthy export trade, proving particularly popular in Germany. The Germans did build their own engines, of which the most popular was the Berliner Maschinenbau. One of the most successful rollers was built by Marshalls of Gainsborough, which was notable for its radial valve gear that made reversing remarkably simple. It comes as quite a surprise to anyone used to other steam engines to find that the reversing lever simply moves with no effort at all from one position to the other, and equally makes it an easy job for the driver to shift from full forward to an intermediate position for efficient running. The Marshall engine had a feedwater pump worked by the crankshaft for refilling the boiler, but even so it had a very limited range of just a few miles, not an important factor when it was rolling a stretch of road, but inconvenient when travelling from place to place. The rollers were so vital to road upkeep that they had a legal right to demand water along the way, and the drivers had keys to water hydrants.

Among the many useful innovations introduced in the early twentieth century was a change in roller construction. Originally, when a roller became worn, the only thing to be done was to replace the whole unit. A new system was introduced in 1910, in which instead of being made of solid metal, the rollers had an outer casing of metal plates that could be replaced. Some manufacturers produced 'convertibles', that could be changed from rollers to conventional traction engines. One change was certainly welcomed by the crew: later rollers were built with a canopy that offered at least some protection from the weather.

In the twentieth century as motor traffic increased, the need for decently surfaced roads became paramount and the rollers had an essential part to play, in both laying new surfaces to replace the old, dusty tracks of a previous generation and in keeping the new roads repaired. Rolling alone was no longer enough. When asphalt or tar roads were being laid, the first job was to break up the old surface. 'Scarifiers' were used – robust toothed attachments that dug into the old surface. Morrison, Allen & Price designed a heavy

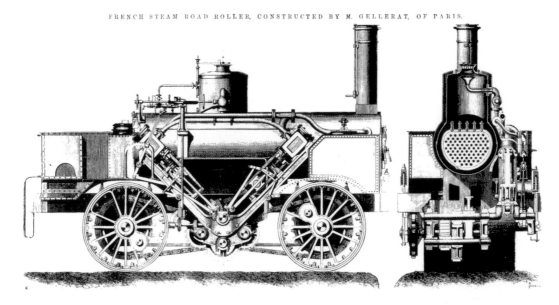

FRENCH STEAM ROAD ROLLER, CONSTRUCTED BY M. GELLERAT, OF PARIS.

This roller built by Gellerae of Paris is quite unlike any other. The inclined cylinders drive onto a common crank and transmission is by chains to both front and back wheels.

roller with spikes that could be attached to the rear axle of the steam roller. It was not able to start straight away in breaking the surface. Holes had to be made in the road with hand picks, and the scarifier manoeuvred into position so that the spike dropped into the holes; after that it could get under way. Many later rollers were fitted with permanent scarifiers that could be lowered into position. At the end of the process, the broken up material was generally shovelled away by hand.

In the early years, the steam roller was virtually the only mechanical device to be seen on a road construction programme. On major works, a temporary depot would be set up on site. Here the hot tar was mixed with gravel to make the 'metal', a filthy job that was done by hand. The hot mixture was then brought, usually on a horse-drawn flat, then it had to be shovelled onto the road surface. After that it had to be raked and rammed down by the men before the roller could start work. In order to keep the tar hot, braziers had to be lit along the sides of the length being worked, and the men were constantly having to heat their shovels and rakes to get rid of accumulations of sticky tar. It was to be some years before tar spraying machines were added to the normal working site.

Fowler produced an interesting version – an engine that could be converted from steam roller to traction engine. This involved exchanging the rollers for wheels. The instructions make it sound quite simple when a jack was available, but distinctly precarious if not. The change started with the back wheels:

'If no jack is available, lay a plank with a wedge below it about 18' long behind each hind roller, and with engine reversed slowly steam on to both planks until sufficiently high to remove both rollers. Pack up under the hind tank and scotch up the front rollers securely, knock out both wedges and planks, when both hind rollers will be left clear of the road for changing.

'When the two traction wheels are in position, insert wedges and planks again, remove scotches from front roller, and steam on to the planks again until the packing is released from below hind tank. Remove this and then steam forward until both wheels are on the ground clear of the planks.'

After that, another complex procedure is required to change the front end. Fowler in their 'Working Instructions for Fowler Road Rollers' from which the above description is taken, also provide hints on some of the special problems associated with the vehicles. For example, when the roller is not fitted with differential gear, they recommend removing the driving pin from the inner wheel when going round a corner, which must have made any long distance travel frustratingly slow. For hilly country, they recommend steel-plated or cast-steel wheels that give better grip than cast iron. Rolling uphill can create problems, pushing the road metal up instead of flattening it out. They suggest rolling half the road

A road gang at work at Olonne-sur-Mer on the west coast of France.

at a time, 'leaving the unmetalled half of the road for the roller to run up on'. Much of the rest of the advice is little different from that which would apply to any type of steam engine. One piece of advice would at least have saved a lot of time and effort – and very early starts to the day. They explain how the fire can be banked up overnight to speed up the process of raising steam the next day. First the steam pressure has top be dropped right down and the boiler filled with water. The ashpan damper and firehole door should be closed and a plate put on top of the chimney.

In the twentieth century, there were to be more changes in design. The Aveling Rochester works used more modern machine tools and the old slide valves on the engines gave way to piston valves. It was also clear that competition was now available in the rapidly developing diesel engines vehicles of all kinds. In order to deal with this, twelve manufacturers got together to do joint marketing under the name Agricultural Engineers Ltd. This alone was not enough, and a new company was formed by amalgamating Aveling with

The Fowler interchangeable system, showing the alternative roller and wheels for the front end that would change the roller into a traction engine.

Barford of Peterborough. The very last steam roller came off the production line in Rochester in 1947.

It is difficult to imagine how our modern road system could have ever been developed without the steam roller. They remained in use well into the second half of the twentieth century and the author remembers as a small boy being really excited when one came to repair a local road. The local kids would gather round and watch and the bolder ones would ask for a ride – they never got one. Local authorities kept them going for a surprisingly long time. Leicestershire County Council only sold off their last three engines in 1960. They were originally intended for scrap, but enthusiasts heard about them and put in offers to buy. One of them went to that wonderful enthusiast for all things steam – Rev. Teddy Boston of Cadeby, where it joined his traction engine *Fiery Elias* and his private light railway. One of the others is the 1920s Marshall now owned by David Hurley and his family and is seen near his home in Lincolnshire (p.83). It is good to see that it and others have survived, even if it is no longer required to roll out tarmac. Its role was taken over by the diesel roller, and one can see the advantages; no need to get up hours ahead of work time to raise steam for a start! The diesel is unquestionably more efficient, but as a small boy I would not have dashed out to see it at work.

CHAPTER SIX

Road Haulage

As we saw in Chapter 2, authorities did not exactly give a wholehearted welcome to the idea of steam being used on the road. Even if there had been more enthusiasm, for most people steam power now meant railways. The great turning point came in 1831 with the opening of the first inter-city line, the Liverpool & Manchester Railway. Its promoters had originally thought of it primarily in terms of carrying freight, much as the canals had been doing for the last half century and more, but passengers loved it. As a result of its success, there was an absolute rush to create new lines all over the country and as more and more lines opened, so the number of passengers carried each year escalated. In 1843 the railways reported carrying some 23 million passengers; just five years later that figure had shot up to nearly 70 million. While the steam carriages were never meant to go much faster than the old horse drawn coaches, the railways were altogether more dashing. Robert Stephenson's famous engine *Rocket*, generally accepted as the forerunner of all later steam locomotives, astonished spectators by dashing along at a brisk 30mph. Thanks to reasonably priced third class tickets, which may not have offered much in the way of comfort to the travelling public, but got them to their destination at the same time as the passengers in first class, railway travel was, it seemed, a possibility for everyone. It is no wonder that investors rushed to buy shares and lost interest in developing passenger traffic on the roads. There was, however, still the question of freight, and here the traction engine had a distinct advantage. It could be taken virtually anywhere, not confined to places where track had been laid.

Legislation worked against the road locomotive in so many ways - restricting speeds to little more than walking pace and, of course, enforcing the notorious Red Flag Act. But there were jobs that traction engines could do where power and versatility were far more important than speed. One of the early builders of road locomotives was Charles Burrell & Sons of Thetford, Norfolk. They had begun building conventional agricultural traction and portable engines in 1848, but when they began constructing their first road engines in 1856 they turned to an idea developed by a British engineer,

James Boydell. He developed what he called an engine with 'endless rails', later known as 'Dreadnought wheels'. Steel boards were fitted to the circumference of the engine's conventional wheels, spreading the weight of the engine, making it far more usable on soft ground. It was to prove its value in industry that had always faced problems getting its product to market; forestry and logging.

Trees are felled in the forest, where the ground is often difficult and for centuries the only way of getting the logs out was to use heavy horses. This was a task ideally suited to the Burrell-Boydell engines.

A magnificent example of a Burrell engine on display at a steam fair in New Zealand.

The huge expansion of the logging industry in the Sierra Nevada, following the Californian gold rush, created a demand for an efficient transport system to get the timber out of the forests. The engine is hauling a most impressive load.

It had already made a slow, lumbering progress from Thetford to Woolwich Arsenal with a load of timber, but it was out in the forest itself that it was to prove most useful. Woodland has always been a difficult terrain as all walkers know. If anywhere is going to be a soggy morass it is on a woodland bridleway, where the shade of the trees prevents quick drying. And if that was not bad enough, most woodland has undergrowth of one sort or another, from young saplings to thorny bushes, and many woods have rocks hidden among ferns and bracken. Getting a tree trunk that might weigh several tons from the spot it was felled to anything like a decent road is always a daunting task; but many of the obstacles that made hard work for horses meant little to a heavy traction engine, especially one fitted with a primitive form of caterpillar track. But road engines of all types were eventually to be used in the logging industry.

One area in which steam proved vital to the development of a major logging industry was the Sierra Nevada. It was the California Gold Rush of 1848 that produced a hugely increased demand for timber – for flues, pit props for mines and for wooden buildings of all kinds. The forests of the Sierra Nevada had the raw material in plenty but the greatest difficulty was transport. The terrain was generally too rugged for horses to work deep in the forest, and the rivers of the region were far too wild to be used for floating the timber out. The answer was to use traction engines and steam tractors to haul out the timber and carry it to the various steam-powered saw mills. They did not, however, have the use of the Burrell type engines and as a result the heavy engines churned up the ground making life difficult for everyone involved. This was equally true of most logging concerns, not merely in the Sierras.

The first problem to overcome was getting the engine to the site of the felled tree as the wheels often got bogged down. In such cases the answer was generally to find a suitably stout tree, fasten ropes round it and attach them to the engine, which could then haul itself forward. Once at the site, the more difficult task had to be faced of moving not just the engine but its load of a massive tree trunk as well. At a difficult site a method known as 'scotching' was used. The engine itself was secured to a tree and heavy baulks of timber placed in front of the wheels to stop it moving. Chains were placed round the trunk, and then attached to wire ropes for haulage – the wire was never placed directly round the trunk, as it would simply bite into the timber and spoil it. In an ideal world, the trunk would be dragged out top first but where that was impossible it came out butt first, which could gouge deep furrows in the ground. Most pulls simply involved hooking the wire rope to the chains and hauling out the timber, but with really massive trunks this was not always possible. In that case the solution was to use blocks, mostly snatch blocks that were simply slid over the wire. There is, of course, a price to pay when using blocks. With a straight pull, if, for example, 16ft of wire is wound onto the drum, then the trunk will move forward by 16ft. But with even the simplest pulley system, drawing in 16ft of wire will only move the trunk by half that distance. Getting a massive trunk out into a clearing where it could be handled more easily was a slow, laborious process.

The problems did not end when the trunk reached the roadway; the surface would not have lasted long if trunks had simply been dragged across it. For the final stage of the journey to the saw mill, the trunks were loaded onto special vehicles, variously known as drags, tugs, carriages or pole wagons. The last name gives more of an idea of how they were constructed. At the front of the vehicle was a steerable bogie, linked to the rear carriage by a long pole. The rear carriage could be adjusted by being moved along the pole to get the best possible weight distribution for a particular load. The timber was rested against a bolster fitted with pins to hold the timber in place. Getting the trunks onto the wagon was no easy matter. The engine was set on one side of the pole wagon and the trunk on the other. Skids of hardwood were placed along the side of the wagon nearest the trunk and wire ropes run from the trunk to the engine. Then the slow job of hauling the timber up the trunk could begin, a job that required a great deal of precision in getting everything properly aligned. The operation was frequently stopped to allow fine adjustments to be made. Once everything was on board and secured the load could finally be hauled away, the simplest part of the whole operation. But it was not all that easy, managing such a long, heavy load on what were often poorly surfaced roads.

Now new problems appeared: the driver had to cope with his long, heavy load. Cornering on sharp bends was especially difficult. The pivoted front wheels on the wagon would be following one curve, while the rear wheels were on a different track. Preventing skidding and slewing required real skill – skill that only came with experience. Hills presented another challenge, particularly downhill sections, where the heavy load would be pushing hard at the engine in front and unless care was taken, the whole outfit would start to run away with itself. Usually a man had to be positioned on the tow to brake it. On some occasions the engine and its load might have to pass through urban areas; one can easily imagine the mayhem that would be caused if the driver got his cornering wrong and the pole wagon swung out in a wide arc, demolishing whatever happened to be in the way. A learner driver might well have collected a few lamp posts before he got the hang of things. Even when the whole outfit reached the saw mill, problems were not over, as space was often limited and manoeuvring difficult. Fortunately, most yards would have had some sort of crane or hoist, which at least made the unloading easier than the loading.

There was an alternative available in some cases, where an engine could be used to work a portable saw bench – bringing the mill to the timber rather than the timber to the mill. This, however, only worked for comparatively simple jobs – for the big timber firms such as those of the Sierra Nevada it was never an option.

Heavy work such as this called for powerful engines and none could match the 150 horsepower engine built by J.L. Case of Wisconsin. The first model was built in 1904 and only a few of these monsters were built. An idea of its power can be gauged by the first test run, when the prototype hauled four conventional traction

This advertisement from an American manufacturer emphasises one of the values of portable engines to the logging industry; it was often cheaper to bring the saw to the timber rather than the timber to a distant mill. In the background one can see a typical locomotive of the mid nineteenth century.

engines with a combined weight of 24 tons up a 13 per cent gradient outside the works. The statistics are equally impressive. Power came from a single 14-inch diameter cylinder engine working at a pressure of 160psi. It was definitely built for power not speed; the two gears gave speeds of just under 6mph in high and 2½mph in low. The huge rear wheels were 8-foot diameter and 30 inches wide and the engine carried 500 gallons of water in the tank and 1200lb of coal, enough to keep the beast going for around three hours. In the event, it was generally thought to be too big and Case settled for more modest, but still imposing, 110 horsepower steam tractors. These were a huge success and 877 of the machines were built. Steam traction had reached a zenith of power.

Legislation was not the only factor that hampered the development of steam road haulage. There was some concern about whether the many bridges in the country could sustain the weight of a heavy engine, a fact that railway companies seem to have made good use of. It is surprising how many signs still exist stating that a bridge is unsuitable for traction engines; the railways never were keen on competition. With new bridges, there was a simple test to apply; run the engines over it and see what happens and the photograph on p.101 shows just such a test being carried out on a new canal bridge. The authorities that owned the various bridges did at least have the knowledge that if things did go wrong they would not bear the expense – that would be down to the owner of the engine that caused the damage. The steam hauliers were not pleased, as one of them wrote at the time:

'If I send a boiler weighing fifteen tons drawn by fifteen horses (weighing eight tons) over a bridge and that boiler breaks then I have nothing to pay, but if I send the same boiler over

This immense Best Co. engine was one of two purchased by the Northern California Power Co. for heavy haulage for the Battle Creek Hydroelectric Scheme.

the bridge drawn by an engine (weighing eight tons) and that
boiler breaks through the bridge, I have the whole expense
to pay'.

One can see that he had a point, though the weight distribution of
fifteen horses is not exactly the same as that of one steam engine.
However, the statement also gives an indication of just why steam
haulage became successful; it assumes that one engine can do the
work of fifteen horses. And that extra power was needed, thanks to
new developments in many industries

The nineteenth century saw machinery getting bigger and bigger,
and nowhere was this more true than in the ship building industry.
The author's great grandfather was one of three Riley brothers who
established their works in Stockton-on-Tees, constructing ships'
boilers. These were not the biggest ever built at that time, but they
were still large. They were certainly too big to be carried by rail
or canal, so they had to be sent to the shipyard by road, and the
company decided that the best means of doing so was by using a
steam tractor. It is interesting to compare the two photos (pp.105
and 107) to see the difference between what one traction engine
could haul and the number of horses needed for a similar task.
Other companies had even bigger items to despatch. The famous
company John Brown had its main yards on the Clyde, but when
they received the order to build the *Lusitania* in 1903, intended to
be one of the fastest and most luxurious liners in the world, many
of the largest castings had to be made at the company's foundry
in Sheffield. They were then sent overland to Glasgow, not always
with the most satisfactory results. As Sir Allan Grant noted in his
history of the company:

'It was a curious thing that when the breakdown of the traction
engines took place, which was a fairly frequent occurrence, they
nearly always happened within a hundred yards or so of the
Snake Inn, or one of the other isolated places of refreshment on
that barren route.'

One cannot blame the men too much – working on a slow moving
engine, open to the elements in that bleak Pennine landscape must
have been arduous – and the opportunity to stop off for a few
pints all but irresistible. It was the owner of a traction engine that
was demonstrating heavy haulage at the Great Dorset Steam Fair,

who summed up what many thought of the engine crews of those days. 'They were men of iron.'

Specific industries had specific problems for which the traction engine provided the best solution. Portland limestone has always been prized and used for some of Britain's most prestigious buildings, such as St. Paul's cathedral. Portland itself was an island just off the Dorset coast until the first bridge joined it to the mainland in the early nineteenth century. Most of the quarrying was carried out high above the tall cliffs, so there was always a major problem in getting the stone down to the quays for shipmen. This involved moving heavy blocks down what were often very steep slopes. The Rev. W. Skelton visited the island in 1804 and described the methods used:

> 'The blocks being placed on a strong wooden carriage, with solid wheels appropriate to the weight they are to sustain, two horses are harnessed one before and one and sometimes two behind; the latter being supplied with strong breeching, in order to act as drawbacks to the carriage, and prevent its running with too great velocity down the steep; indeed the sagacity and exertions of these poor animals in this arduous employment, is really astonishing; they squat down on their haunches, and suffer themselves to be dragged for many yards, struggling with all their strength against the weight that forces them forwards. To one unaccustomed to the sight, it appears as though their limbs must inevitably dislocated, or their sinews cracked by the violence of their exertions.'

No doubt the decision to replace horses by traction engines was mainly made for economic reasons, but it would also have relieved a great deal of animal suffering. The dangers of the load running away were all too obvious – and they did not end when traction engines took over the work of the horses. In July 1921 George White was driving a Fowler engine with a huge load of stone when a pinion broke. With no means of controlling the descent, the load hurtled forwards, crushing the driver to death. Traction engines continued in use on Portland up to 1931. Today stone is still worked here, but the only reminder of the days of steam is an old portable engine, last seen slowly rusting away in one of the abandoned quarries.

The value of the traction engine became more and more appreciated as it came into more general use. The early years of

In Britain, there was always concern over whether or not bridges were capable of carrying the heavy loads of the steam age. The authorities decided that the best way to test this new canal bridge was to put as many heavy vehicles on it as they could; it is not clear whether the gentleman in the bath chair is part of the load or merely a spectator.

railway mania had subsided and with their passing the enthusiasm for building expensive branch lines never likely to show a profit seeped away, leaving many rural areas with nothing better than a horse and cart to meet their transport needs. The fears that steam would frighten the horses also diminished, as anyone near a railway station could see for themselves that the vast majority of animals regarded steam locomotives with calm equanimity. Even the law began to recognise that 'frightening the horses' was more myth than reality. In his 1869 autobiography, Richard Tangye, founder of a famous firm of steam engine manufacturers – he could hardly have been anything else, since his middle name was Trevithick – wrote with obvious pleasure about a court case. 'A judge ruled that a horse that would not stand the sight and sound of a locomotive, in these days of steam, constituted a public danger, and that its owner should be prosecuted and not the owner of the locomotive. In this case, sadly, the judiciary proved more radical than the legislature'. This was certainly true, as Tangye's book was published just four years after the passing of the Red Flag Act.

There was a gradual easing of the regulations. The Highways and Locomotives (Amendment) Act of 1878 removed the restrictions on such vital factors as the permissible weight of traction engines and the permitted width of tyres. It was also no longer necessary for engines to 'consume their own smoke', which had effectively forced them to use coke as a fuel. This encouraged manufacturers to build heavier and more powerful engines – engines that could take on far greater loads. It was not, however, until the passing of the Locomotives on Highways Act of 1896 that real change came about – including raising the speed limit to 12mph and getting rid of the infamous red flag. The Act was less the result of lobbying by the steam fraternity than the result of the increasing popularity of the new internal combustion motor cars. The passing of the Act was celebrated by a procession of vehicles travelling between London and Brighton in what was to become a popular annual event for vintage and veteran vehicles of all kinds.

With the increase in demands being made on traction engines for heavy haulage, there was a need to supply more power. One way of doing this was to use compound steam engines, with high and low pressure cylinders. This compound traction engine was built by Aveling and Porter.

The various Acts gave extra powers to local authorities to improve roads as more and more of the old Turnpike Trusts disappeared from the scene. That did not, however, mean that they necessarily took advantage of the provisions to do anything very much. As a result, designers of traction engines had to come up with ways of overcoming the problems of travelling on rough, pot-holed surfaces. The obvious first stage was to do something about springing on the engines. There was no real difficulty with engines that used a chain drive, but there were problems when power was transmitted through gears. Some arrangement had to be included so that the up and down motion of the main axle as the engine bounced its way down a rough road did not affect the gears, putting them out of alignment. Different manufacturers found different solutions to the problem.

Aveling and Porter, for example, used an ingenious arrangement for their gears, by which the main spur wheel was encased in a rigid tube, the large end of which was secured to the horn plate. As a result the gears were always kept in pitch, regardless of any movement of the axle. The springs to either side of the engine worked independently. Fowler road engines had the main weight at the back of the engine resting on very strong plate springs, while a system of suspension hooks and equalising levers ensured the gearing remains undisturbed. The springs at the front of the engine were situated above the axle.

American manufacturers often developed different ideas on springing. J.L. Case, responsible for some of the largest traction engines ever built, used spiral springs that supported the entire weight of the engine, so that on a bumpy road the boiler would move up and down. Compensating links were used to keep the gears in train. Foden had their own arrangement, patented in 1892, which they claimed to be ideal:

'This perfect spring arrangement materially reduces the effect of shocks or vibrations caused by passing over rough roads, and it is conducive to the reduction of the wear and tear arising from such causes in ordinary traction engines, as leaky fire-boxes, tubes and joints, strained frames, and the jolting to pieces of the motion work throughout. Moreover, this spring mounting arrangement adds very considerably to the comfort of the engine-driver and steersman.'

One suspects that the potential benefits to the engine crew were not the first priority, given that most of them were required to work without any protection from the weather.

Another area that could be investigated to make travel easier was the cladding for the wheels. A new type of wheel was developed by McLaren and J.W.Boulton and manufactured by McLaren and Aveling & Porter. It consisted of a cast iron wheel, with slots around the perimeter. Hard wood blocks were fitted loosely into these cells with the end of the block slightly protruding from the rim, with the inner end of the block resting on a pad. As the wheel rotates, pressure forces the lower blocks down onto the road surface. This makes for a smooth ride and the engines were also welcomed by road authorities as they did no damage to paving setts. This certainly contrasts with the standard Case traction engine, which, because it was mainly intended for use on soft ground, had iron spikes round the rim of the drive wheel.

There were many different methods tried throughout the nineteenth century to improve the grip of the wheel on the road and to ease out bumps and hollows on the surface. The final solution to the problem was only arrived at after a series of trials and experiments. A naturally occurring product that combined strength with elasticity was rubber, which had first been introduced into Europe from South America in the seventeenth century, when Spanish settlers used it to line their cloaks to make them waterproof. Over the next couple of hundred years, manufacturing techniques improved, but the rubber they produced suffered from a serious disadvantage that made it unsuitable for possible use as a tyre material: it could turn hard and inelastic in very cold weather and soften and even melt in hot weather. This meant that many goods that had been put on the market caused a great deal of dissatisfaction among customers and many new companies that had entered into the industry were going bankrupt. One man made it his objective to overcome these problems: he was a former hardware merchant from Philadelphia, Charles Goodyear.

Goodyear's task was far from straightforward and he had many setbacks, but he kept trying new variations and eventually he decided to try an experiment, heating the rubber with sulphur and white lead. At first it seemed no more successful than any other method, but one day he overheated one specimen and produced charring but did not melt the rubber – and the border that had not

In the nineteenth century, the shipping industry began to turn away from sail to steam, and this required the construction of more and more heavy equipment. Riley Brothers of Stockton-on-Tees manufactured large boilers, one of which is seen here being moved from the works by traction engine.

been charred had been perfectly cured. He repeated the process with an open fire and once again he produced a substance that was exactly what he had been looking for: rubber that neither hardened in the cold nor softened in the heat. He patented the process in America in 1841 and applied for a patent in England three years later. Unfortunately for Goodyear, John Hancock, who had been working on rubber manufacture for some years, had discovered a similar process, and already had a patent by 1843. It was obvious to many that this new substance presented real possibilities for development to all kinds of new uses. The first to think about making rubber tyres was Robert Thompson.

His first attempt was a pneumatic tyre, patented in 1845. This consisted of an inner tube made up of a number of inflated cells, made out of calico coated in rubber. They were held in place by an outer case of leather and canvas. It was not a success. He then decided to try a simpler method: coating a wheel with indiarubber. This was also a failure, but Thompson persevered. His main problem was that the rubber he was using was simply too soft, and on really hot days it became quite tacky and tended to stick to the road. He then tried a harder rubber and finally felt the time had come to test the new tyres on an actual vehicle. He built what he described as a 'light tractor', though weighing in at five tons it was only light in comparison with more conventional traction engines. Now a new problem appeared: the rubber tended to stretch in the heat and come away from the rim. This produced the novel sight on a hot day of the wheels spinning merrily, while the tyres remained stuck and the vehicle was equally immobilised.

Thompson was undeterred; he began constructing light, three-wheeled tractors, which, while they were greeted with little enthusiasm in Britain, found markets overseas, including in India. The original version had a vertical boiler, but later versions built by Burrell with more conventional horizontal boilers. Nevertheless, the idea of a three-wheeled engine that could be made quite compact by the use of a vertical boiler did catch on. Among those who produced a vehicle of the sort were the British company Catley & Ayres. Where Thompson had only thought in terms of a tractor for haulage, they built a passenger wagonette that was given its first outing at the Yorkshire Agricultural Society show in 1871. It took four passengers on a trip round York at speeds of up to twenty miles an hour. Catley later commented, 'the horses they met during their numerous journeys took no notice of it'. Thompson's perseverance did eventually pay off, and solid rubber tyres became commonplace on traction engines. All these developments resulted in a steady improvement in traction engine design and increased its importance in the world of transport, but there were always some problems that had to be overcome once they were set to work.

William Fletcher in his book on traction engine published in 1904 described some of the problems facing engine drivers – and also on the need to build engines with great strength. He dwelt at some length on the difficulties that might be faced when driving over bad roads or taking threshing machines onto land 'little better than swamps'. But the worst conditions were usually met on country roads:

'During wet weather the narrow lanes are so soft that there is a strong probability of seeing the engine gently slide into a country ditch, or suddenly sink into a bog, the rest of a rainy day being often spent by the men in charge in endeavouring to extricate the

engine by the aid of planks, screw-jacks, hurdles, and anything available. All the parts must be strong enough to bear the enormous strain of such an emergency as the engine lifting itself out of this hole or ditch, so that an ample margin of strength is absolutely necessary.'

He goes on to point out that the engine also has to be strong enough to cope with mistreatment by negligent drivers, who enthusiastically grease and oil the parts they can easily reach – and neglect others that are hard to get at – even if their smooth working is essential for keeping the engine in good condition. One area that was perhaps more difficult to reach was the gearing, especially with inside gearing, which had become far more popular by the end of the nineteenth century, for both smoother and quieter working. Traction engines were generally fitted up with just the two gear positions – slow and fast, though 'fast' was scarcely an accurate description of traction engine travel. The biggest change in construction came in the latter part of the nineteenth century with the general availability of good quality steel. The later engines were also fitted with differential gears, mainly fitted to the main axle. This arrangement compensated for the fact that when turning

The contrast between steam power and horse power is dramatically demonstrated in this photograph, where an immense team of horses is needed to move this massive anchor from an ironworks in Dudley in the Black Country.

The Island of Portland is famous for its limestone quarries. Until the steam age all the huge blocks of stone had to be moved by horses, which put great strain on the animals as they coped with the steep slopes from the quarries to the quays. Here the job is done efficiently by traction engine.

a tight corner, one of the driving wheels on the inside of the curve will be travelling faster than the one on the outside. This both made steering easier and reduced wear and tear.

A number of manufacturers introduced compound engines at the end of the nineteenth century. Steam pressure had been increased over the years – most boilers would have been water-tested up to 250psi, well above the normal working pressure. But with a pressure of a large engine being perhaps 180psi. the exhaust steam would still be under pressure when it left the cylinder, so instead of allowing it to simply be blown away as exhaust steam, it could be passed to a second cylinder. To allow for the lower pressure, the second cylinder would be of larger diameter than the first high-pressure cylinder. Compound engines had been built for stationary engines at least a century earlier, but were only slowly adopted for traction engines.

The traction engine proved itself to be a robust vehicle, capable of working in difficult conditions for long periods of time. J & H McLaren made something of a speciality in building engines for use overseas, where conditions were often far from favourable. The engines specifically designed for South Africa, were compounds, with 7-inch high pressure and 12inch low pressure cylinders that developed 70 brake horse power and were tested hauling a 55 ton load up a 1 in 12 slope. They were built with very wide drive wheels to cope with soft ground, and unlike most engines of the day used a worm and rack steering system instead of chains. This was thought to be more reliable, a feature that would certainly be required when, as was often the case, they were required to travel on narrow mountain roads. They did indeed prove themselves remarkably resilient. An engine used for wool carriage in New Zealand was recorded as having covered 70,000 miles without ever breaking a spring.

Traction engines were called on to move ever bigger loads and the development of electric power brought fresh challenges. Moving generating equipment from the manufacturer to the power station was always an immense task. Cochrane and Co. had been building ship's boilers at Birkenhead, but later moved to Annan in Dumfries & Galloway. This was convenient for ship builders, but there was a growing demand for steam accumulators for various industries and these could be very imposing bits of equipment. When they received an order for an accumulator from Glasgow they decided to despatch it by road using a single engine, even though the item was around seventy foot long and weighed 90 tons – and the total load with the trailer and equipment probably added another twenty tons to the load. The machine that undertook the 80-mile journey now has its place in history as having the honour of hauling the heaviest load ever moved by a single engine. There is no monument to Fowler 'Super Lion, no. 1705 'Atlas', but perhaps there should be.

Cochrane's were involved in what turned out to be the ultimate marathon of the steam age. The company had received an order for two of their massive boilers from a gas works in London's dockland. They were each similar in size to the Glasgow accumulator – 70-foot long by 12-foot diameter. Moving such monsters required specialist knowledge and the contract went to the most experienced hauliers in Britain – Pickfords. The company was begun by James Pickford in 1756 in the era of horse and cart, but they prided themselves on always being in touch with all the latest changes in transport technology. When the canal age got under way they bought a fleet of boats, but sold them off and moved on to steam in the nineteenth century. So they were the ideal firm to take on this journey of over three hundred miles, often over very difficult terrain. You cannot just set out with a load this size and hope for the best; there were many towns along the route whose narrow, twisty streets could not cope with it and for which alternative diversions had to be found. A full eighteen months was taken up with planning; going over the whole ground, to make sure the journey could actually be made. Bridges had to be tested to make sure they could carry the weight – and in some cases specially strengthened from below. Local authorities had to be consulted and the police involved. Given that the speed allowed for the journey was a tortoise-paced two miles an hour, this was going to cause huge problems for other road users. A special trailer had to be built by Crane of Dereham, Norfolk that was carried on a pair of bogeys each mounted on 16 wheels.

The date set for the start of the journey was 6 January 1938, when conditions could hardly have been ideal. A week before the start a team set out to go over the whole route again to make sure there had been no changes and that all necessary strengthening work had been carried out. Three Fowler engines were involved on this occasion; Ajax again and No. 16263 Talisman were responsible for moving the load and 16264 Jix followed on with the living van for the crew and was required to help out the other two in especially difficult circumstances. Those circumstances were encountered early in the drive when the engines had to cross the notorious Shap Fell with a summit 1500 feet above sea level. One can have some idea of the difficulties of crossing this bleak moorland when one thinks that at this date banking engines were still in use over Shap to help out with even powerful locomotives on the nearby railway. In the event the crew were faced with heavy snowfalls, and Jix was kept just as busy as the other two engines. It was not just a question of helping haul the load up to the summit; it also had to be placed at the back of the load to help with braking on the slippery, slithering downhill run. There were other problems along the way: at sharp bends the team had to lay down metal sheets to provide a surface for the wheels and on many occasions, they had to get out saws to deal with overhanging branches.

The whole team finally emerged at the outskirts of London after three weeks on the road and now they had to pause. The only way they could be allowed to pass through the crowded city streets was to travel by night and special arrangements were made for the last leg of the journey. To ensure they always had water for the boiler a 3,000 gallon water tank was towed along with the load, and the speed was increased to something more

like walking pace – a steady 3mph. It went without a hitch and the job was completed. All the men had to do now was turn round and go all the way back again.

The Cochrane load was an exceptional one and Pickfords normal everyday business was very different. They had finally abandoned their canal trade in 1848, selling off the last of their narrow boats as the future would rely largely on moving goods by rail. They established furniture stores, known as pantechnicons – a word originally used to mean a bazaar crammed full of works of art. They ordered special pantechnicon vans, but over time the word 'van' was dropped and a pantechnicon became a vehicle instead of a storehouse. Originally the pantechnicons, simple high-sided four-wheelers, with low floors for easy loading, were worked by horses and were used to move goods between a store and the nearest station. But railway transport did have problems. In the early years, trucks were loose coupled, so that when a locomotive stopped, the trucks and vans behind it kept on moving, crashing into each other until the whole train came to rest. This was not ideal if you

It was not only horses that had problems with the steep roads of Portland. In July 1921 this engine crashed, killing the driver, George White.

were responsible for moving a family's cherished crockery and glassware. Pickfords turned back to using road transport just as they had two centuries before, but this time with a fleet of traction engines to do the work. As it was mostly fairly straightforward, comparatively light work, they relied mainly on 8hp Fowlers.

One of the busiest hauliers of the period was Lalonde Brothers & Parham of Weston-Super-Mare, later of Bristol. They were early enthusiasts for steam and, like Pickfords, turned to Fowler's for their engines. Unfortunately, things did not work out well. The company decided they knew more about steam engine technology than the engineers and informed Fowler's that they should make their fireboxes larger. Fowler's disagreed and the hauliers ordered a new engine from Garrett to their own specification. It made its debut in 1908 and became known as the Garrett No.6 Express or the Garrett Lalonde. Whether it was down to Garrett themselves or interference from Lalonde, the engine was not a success. It suffered badly from overheating and cracked crankshafts. Rather humiliatingly, the company had to go back to Fowler's and accept the engines they had previously rejected. The only people who benefited from the fiasco were the lawyers who sorted out the various contracts and the compensation claims. In spite of that experience, the Lalonde brothers became founding members of the National Traction Engine Owners Association.

The companies who organised the hauls are often known, but we rarely get to hear the names of those who did the actual work. Nor do we find many records of exactly what was involved in travelling long distances on uncovered engines while hauling loads big and small. Even those of us lucky enough to have spent some time with these splendid machines can only get a very rough estimate of what conditions must have been like a hundred years ago, working long hours and travelling over often inadequate roads.

It is an occasional irritation to motorists in a hurry to find themselves following a gently puffing engine down the road, but in the days when these engines were regularly at work they might have proved even more irritating. It is only surprisingly well into the twentieth century that the law decreed that in Britain vehicles should stick to the left hand side of the road – though they were advised to move to one side if confronted with something coming the other way. Before that, traction engines preferred to stick to the middle. There was a good reason for this: the roads of the time had a very distinct camber, so that there was always a tendency to slip

A fine array of American traction engines at a steam fair.

sideways if straying far from the centre in wet or icy conditions. This was particularly important for the furniture removers, whose engines often had to pull a string of pantechnicons behind them. This was a job that required careful management.

The last van in the procession was expected to perform much the same task as the brake van on a goods train. Looking after it was always the job of the youngest member of the team, often a young lad. Communication between the driver at the front and the lad at the back was somewhat haphazard, often relying on nothing more complex than a jerk on a string stretched out down the train of vans. The boy as well as helping with braking was also expected to deal with such commonplace occurrences as overheated axle bearings. Inevitably the lad was given the jobs that no one else wanted: being first up in the morning to light the fire in the firebox and raise steam; be last at night to clean the boiler tubes, do the ashing out and top up with water for the next day.

The working days were long and the drivers were expected to cover an appropriate number of miles per day. If one looks at that epic run from Annan to London, then if the crew covered 320 miles in 21 days at 2mph. then they must have been travelling an average of nearly 8 hours a day, which in early January would have meant starting at dawn and ending as dusk fell. Even those figures assume they did not stop for meal breaks or indeed for anything else. Drivers could, of course, occasionally flout regulations. A Lalonde driver was making an appropriately measured pace down a hill, while towing two vans, when he was overtaken by a second engine, also with two vans. The second had put the engine out of gear and was freewheeling down the hill at speed. Needless to say, had he been caught doing this he would almost certainly have been looking for a new job.

The greatest problem affecting haulage in Britain was undoubtedly the attitude of the government, which continued to regard steam on the road as an unwelcome intrusion into the old order. It was not the same in all other countries. In France, the government was actually enthusiastic to embrace the new technology. They ordered three engines from McLaren to run the postal service between Lyon and Grenoble in 1886. In order to be able to make the 112 km (70-mile) journey in a single day the engines would need to travel

The Catley wagonette, with its distinctive vertical boiler, was one of the earliest machines to be fitted with the newly invented rubber tyres.

a great deal faster than the limits set in Britain and the speed limit was set at 12 km an hour. Meanwhile, back in Britain, the gradual easing of regulations still left them far behind the French laws. There were, however, sometime difficulties in enforcing the rules. There was an entertaining incident at Tonbridge in Kent, when an engine was puffing through the town, emitting such vast clouds of smoke that it was almost lost from view. Enough of the machine was visible for the local police sergeant to take down its registration number. When the case came to court, the sergeant was asked why he had not pursued the engine then and there, to which he replied that the engine could travel at 5mph, but he could only manage two, which greatly amused the court. But the sergeant then made the point that the sight of a uniformed officer of the law running down the street would have been hopelessly undignified – which must have been good news for any criminals trying to escape arrest. The magistrates were not amused. On the whole the bench was made up of local gentry, conservative horse riding traditionalists. It was typical of their attitude that a magistrate trying a case in Hythe, publicly described traction engines as 'horrible things' and promptly found against the unfortunate owners.

In most European countries, traction engines were competing with the railways for haulage contracts. In India, however, railways had been comparatively slow to develop – while traffic on the roads was often limited to lumbering bullock carts. One man who had a very different idea was an officer in the Rifle Brigade,

J & H McLaren were very successful in building traction engines for export. This engine with its load of wool bales is at work in New Zealand. The engines proved remarkably robust

Rookes Evelyn Belle Crompton. He had an interesting early life. Born near Thirsk in Yorkshire in 1845 he was taken at the age of six to the Great Exhibition in the Crystal Palace; it had a profound effect on him, even at that young age:

> 'For me the unforgettable part of the whole exhibition was the Machinery Hall … neither Koh-I-Noor diamond nor Osler's crystal fountain had any attractions for me to compare with those of the locomotives, with their brilliantly polished piston rods and brasses burnished like gold.'

His education was not exactly conventional. At the age of eleven he interrupted his schooling to visit the Crimea to see his brother who had fought in the war there. On his return, he went to Harrow, where his interest in science and engineering were undimmed. He constructed a static electric generator to do experiments and also built a model traction engine the Blue Belle. On leaving school he went to work at the Great Northern Railway works at Doncaster, but the fascination with the military that had been with him since his visit to the Crimea gave him a change of direction and he joined the army in 1864, eventually making his way to India. It was

American engines often seem huge by British standards. Here it is being used to help with a sugar beet harvest.

there that he came up with his plan for a road locomotive. There had just been a major effort to improve communications between Delhi and the Punjab with the construction of the Great Trunk Road – and it seemed to him the perfect location for a new form of road transport – the 'Government Steam Train' All he needed was a suitable engine, which was to use a novel type of boiler invented by a Scots engineer, William Thompson. It offered an early form of super heating, by having two boilers, one inside the other – the outer supplying steam to the inner. The shape of the inner portion gave them their popular name of 'pot boilers'.

The engine *Chenah* was to be built by Ransome of Ipswich but there was a problem with raising sufficient steam pressure, as the lack of cheap coal in India meant that it would have to be wood fired. Crompton himself took an active part in the trials. The first few were unsatisfactory so it was decided that the only solution was to increase the blast to the fire and new experiments began. The engine was sent for a trial run at Ipswich racecourse. The increased blast certainly had an effect: it was so powerful that once the engine got under way there was an alarming eruption of red hot cinders blowing out of the chimney. The result was disastrous: the main grandstand was set on fire. In spite of this unpromising start, trials with *Chenah* continued, but as the report from another engine driver in *The Engineer* for 1871 reported the problems with the blast had certainly not yet been solved. The first engine had run short of water and they found a suitable source in an old lady's garden:

'The hose was then popped into the old lady's well, without asking her consent. In a minute a good stream was pouring into our tank. It was not until we had got all the water required that our confiding hostess found that we had pumped her well dry. After this discovery it became expedient that we should proceed as quickly as possible … At 8.15 we passed Burrell's locomotive … and availed ourselves of the opportunity to extinguish the lagging of Chenah's boiler, which had taken fire at the smokebox. Thompson's pot boiler is the best I ever saw for burning of lagging … I may add here that the way in which Lieut. Crompton took his engine over heaps of stones by the roadside and into complicated holes and trenches when passing other engines was sufficient to startle weak nerves. I began to think that the Chenah had been designed for la chasse.'

Not surprisingly, Burrell soon reverted to the more conventional locomotive-type boiler. Eventually the road train went into service in India. Crompton wrote enthusiastically, 'though our loaded train weighed over forty tons, we were making speeds well over twenty – probably nearer thirty – miles an hour.' Crompton abandoned his interest in steam transport and on leaving the army and returning to Britain, he became a pioneer in developing electric lighting.

Crompton was also an enthusiastic advocate for the use of traction engines as military transport. Special engines were designed by Fowler and tested by the Royal Engineers in the early 1880s, engines that became known as 'Sappers'. After the First Boer War, when it became clear that conflict was about to break out again, a special unit was set up, headed by Lt. Col. James Templer, who was given the imposing title – Director of Steam Road Transport. The Sappers proved their worth and by the end of the war in 1902, there were 46 traction engines at work in South Africa. The Fowlers were able to run at speeds up to twelve miles an hour, and Templer described their performance in his own book *Steam Transport on Roads*. 'At present, a train of wagons can, on the best roads, only traverse fifteen to twenty while a traction engine would in the same time reel off sixty to seventy miles a day'. He went on to expand on the work that the steam engines had been doing, with various examples – arguments that could as easily be applied to any form of steam haulage:

> 'The steam horse consumes only cheap coal or wood, while animal muscles must be renewed with expensive hay and oats. At the halt the engine ceases to require fuel and water, whereas horses require food and water in the same quantity as when on the march. When the engine does not work it does not eat, and is costing nothing. Again, the horses would be very much harassed with a continuous march, whereas the capabilities of the steam locomotive are, at least, an average of fifty miles per day, for month after month. The steam sapper 'Queen' came from Chatham to Aldershot, viz. seventy-two miles, in twenty-six hours, and went on its regular work the next morning.'

But running a traction engine for heavy haulage was never a straightforward business. Fowler produced a series of 'Additional Working Instruction' specifically dealing with the problems that might occur. Although purely practical, they conjure up a vivid

picture of just how hard life could be out on the road with heavy loads. And the many different obstacles that had to be overcome. The first thing they stressed was the importance of fully researching the route before setting out, starting with local authority by-laws. The most likely problems would come with bridges, especially old or wooden ones. With the former it might sometimes be necessary to detach the trailer and its load, drive the engine over the bridge and then winch the load over separately. The load on wooden bridges could always be spread by laying extra planks for the engine to drive across. This was still a time, when a number of rivers still had to be crossed by means of fords, in which case a pair of engines might be needed. The one to be hauled across had to have its fire dropped and the boiler given time to cool down before being winched over.

Boggy ground presented a new set of difficulties. The first solution would be to add 'spuds' to the wheels. These are generally hard wooden blocks about four inches thick that can be attached to the rear wheels for extra traction. If that fails, then the crew are in for a spot of hard work. The ground would have to be dug away in front of the engine, and brushwood or branches laid down to provide grip for the spuds. If all else fails with a single engine, a rope has to be taken from the forward winding gear and attached

This compound traction engine by the Russell Co. of America is notable for the very large cabin. This was essential in a country with huge variations in weather conditions.

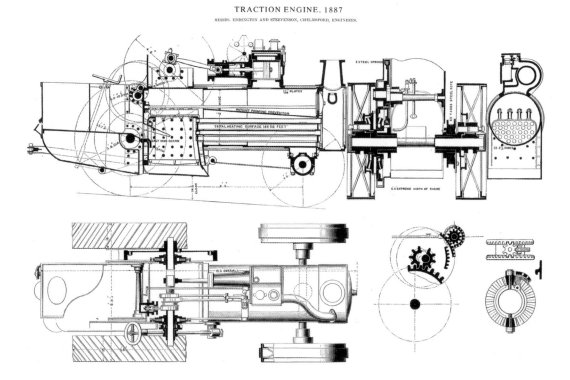

TRACTION ENGINE, 1887

MESSRS. EDDINGTON AND STEEVENSON, CHELMSFORD, ENGINEERS.

This series of diagrams from *The Engineer* of a traction engine built by Eddington and Stevenson of Chelmsford gives an excellent representation of the various working parts of a typical late nineteenth century engine.

to something suitably solid such as a stout tree so that the engine can wind itself out of the mire.

The most common problem facing drivers of heavy loads was provided by steep hills. Going up a hill, the recommendation is to leave the load at the bottom, and once the engine has reached the top, winch it up. Someone has to walk beside the wagons in case the engine cannot manage the task, ready to apply the brake or scotch the wagon to prevent an accident. Descending was rather more perilous. The driver had to ensure that he kept a low fire and that there was enough water in the boiler to keep the top of the firebox covered. All the brakes should be put on before starting the descent, and it should be moved forward slowly, using the reversing gear to keep control. If it did start to run away, the best solution was simply to run the engine into the bank and wait for help. Life on the road was, it seems, never simply a straightforward case of driving from A to B.

The traction engine became a familiar presence on the roads of many countries. They survived in good part because of their durability. Fowler quoted a testimonial from 'A Scottish Newspaper' of 1907, telling the tale of on particular engine:

'There may at present be seen in the neighbourhood of Novar Station little 4 h.p. Traction Engine which certainly has a history worth recording.

Originally it belonged to the late Duke of Sutherland, and was used and driven personally by him in connection with reclamation works at Lairg many years ago, the builders being John Fowler & Co. Ltd, of Leeds, a firm whose reputation as engineers is world-wide.

'Thirty years ago the engine was purchased by John Macdonald Ltd., and was for a considerable time used by this firm for haulage purposes, and afterwards as a Road Roller! It was then sold to Mr. Hugh Barron, timber merchant, Nairn, who ran it for 16 years; the present owners bought it some time ago. When it is stated that despite its age, the engine had still its original firebox and boiler, and that it is running quite as well as in its earlier days, it will be admitted that it is indeed "A bit of good stuff" and a standing – or, perhaps, we should say a moving – testimony to the surpassing excellence of John Fowler & Co. Lt., as engine builders.'

This is an extraordinary testimony for an engine that seems to have had something like half a century of a busy working life. Yet it was probably far from unique. Traction engines such as this were doing the rather mundane jobs of moving objects around the country. They were essentially workhorses, built to do a job with little regard for fripperies of appearance. There was, however, one class of engine that represented a quite different approach.

Chapter Seven

The Fun of the Fair

British Fairs have their origin in customs that go back many centuries. Hiring fairs were established in the fourteenth century, following the devastation of the Black Death. Originally held each November, employers would meet with workers looking for a job and they would then be signed up for the whole of the next year. Different classes of workers wore emblems on their coats, indicating what their trade was. These were known as 'mops' – hence the alternative name of 'mop fair'. There were also fairs in which produce was sold at particular times of year, of which the best known is the Nottingham Goose Fair, which has been in existence for around 700 years. In spite of its name, it did not necessarily specialise in geese – all kinds of farm produce would be on sale. Different fairs took place in different towns and villages all over the country, but they all had one thing in common: they attracted huge crowds. And where huge crowds gather there is an opportunity for someone to make money, and one way to do this was to offer some form of entertainment. Although some fairs retained the essential element of buying and selling, if not of hiring – the Appleby Horse Fair is an example – for most people the only fair they know is the fun fair.

Jacob Studt's Steam Circus illustrated in the Burrell catalogue for 1909. The rather plain engine at the front of the procession is the only one in use; the other vehicles are all horse drawn. This is one of the few photographs that actually includes a man with a red flag, seen standing by the engine.

The fun fair developed over the years, and was no longer limited to special days of the year. It took on a life of its own. There were sideshows of all kinds and rides. These were limited by the lack of power. Simple roundabouts were pushed round by hand; swing boats were worked by the paying customers, pulling on ropes. A more sophisticated form of roundabout was developed in 1832, which worked by gears and was cranked round by a man turning a handle in the middle of the ride. The early version featured horses, and roundabouts of this kind became known as gallopers. The rides were quite sizeable and the showmen had to take them round the country in horse-drawn wagons, while they themselves and their families lived in caravans, usually referred to as living vans. The arrival of steam power changed everything. The gallopers could be turned by steam engine instead of hand crank and exotic swing boats could be worked by a small donkey engine. The first use of a traction engine for haulage, however, seems not to have been with a travelling fair but with the other popular entertainment of the day, the circus.

Jim Myers was an American circus owner who brought his show to Folkestone in August 1859. The arrival of a circus was in itself a big event in the town, a chance to see exotic animals walking through the streets, while clowns and acrobats showed off their acts. On this occasion, there was a new element to the procession: at the front was a solitary Bray traction engine, lending a hand with the haulage. The idea did not really catch on with circus owners, partly due to the cost but also to some extent because they were worried about the effect of the noise, smoke and steam on their travelling menagerie. And there was also the very practical point that many of the animals used in the acts were capable of pulling a van or waggon. There was, however, at this stage, nothing to distinguish this engine from any other built at the time, but there were changes looming on the horizon, which initially had nothing to do with fairs and circuses, but which take us into the realms of science.

The early nineteenth century was a time when there was a great deal of interest in magnetism and electricity, though at first they did not appear to be connected in any way. As early as 1799 Alessandro Volta had developed a device that came to be known as a Voltaic pile, that consisted of alternate discs of silver and zinc, separated by cardboard soaked in brine. When a wire was attached to the ends of the pile, a steady electric current flowed through it. In effect he had invented what we now call a battery, and his name is still remembered in the electric unit the Volt. It became something of a popular attraction in itself, and people paid to see demonstrations – they were even willing to link hands and receive a collective shock. Others now began serious experimenting with electric currents. In 1832 Michael Faraday demonstrated that a wire carrying an electric current could be forced to move round a fixed magnet, and conversely, that a magnet could be made to move round an electric wire. It was the basis of the electric motor, though no one saw that at the time. He later wondered if by moving a magnet within a coil of wire he could induce an electric current in the wire; in fact, it was the relative movement that produced the effect. This was to be the basis of the electric generator, but once again few people appreciated the significance of what had been done. William Gladstone asked Faraday what possible use this electricity was. The scientist obviously appreciated the political mind and produced the perfect answer, 'Why sir, there is every probability that you will soon be able to tax it.' All this may seem a bit remote from the fun of the fair, but there was one more scientific invention that made electricity not just taxable but highly desirable.

A splendid Burrell showman's engine that is far more elaborate than the one seen in the previous illustration. It has all the features one expects to find; the barley sugar supports for the canopy, the name of the ride and the dynamo immediately above the number plate.

Electric lighting was first developed when it was noticed that when two carbon electrodes were brought close together, a brilliant spark would pass between them. This was the basis for the arc lamp, which proved very useful in such big installations as lighthouses, but was not much use on a smaller scale. But in the 1880s, Joseph Swan in Britain and Thomas Edison in America simultaneously and quite independently developed the familiar filament light bulb. Here was something with many applications, and showmen were quick to see the possibilities of flooding their fairs with brilliant lights at night time. And thanks to the developments that began with Faraday, there was an obvious means of supplying the electricity, no matter where the fair was pitched. All that a generator needed was another source of power to move the magnet in relation to a coil of wire. The earliest power stations used steam power to move their generators, but it did not have to be an engine fixed in one place. You could use the power of a traction engine to turn a dynamo.

The first to develop the traction engine for electrical generation was the man whom we have already met, experimenting with road trains, R.E.B. Crompton. He was able to turn the generating gear over by means of a belt round the flywheel – just as a similar arrangement had much earlier been used to turn the mechanism of a threshing engine. He took the idea to Marshalls of Gainsborough, who attached the dynamo to one of their traction engines and took it off to the Henley Regatta on the Thames for a trial run. The regatta, although ostensibly all about rowing, had also been a big social occasion with partying going on late into the night – now the revellers could party lit by electricity.

The idea of lighting fairgrounds at night with electricity was immediately appealing, but the first efforts were really rather tentative. The first attempt was made using a portable engine that was towed onto the site to work a separate generator. Having to move two units was clearly uneconomical and Thomas Green of Leeds and Savage of King's Lynne produced 'electric light engines' in which the engine and dynamo were mounted on the same chassis. This had the added advantage that the connection between engine and generator did not have to be adjusted every time they were moved – they were always set in the same fixed position. Even so, it must have been obvious that, when traction engines were so well established, it made little sense to revert to the use of portable engines that had to be moved either by a horse or another steam engine. Thomas Aveling had railed against the absurdity of horses pulling steam engines decades ago and now Aveling and Porter came up with a traction engine that had a dynamo mounted above the movement and driven through gearing. But it was another company, Burrell, who came up with a simpler idea that soon became generally accepted. They mounted the dynamo on a bracket in front of the chimney and drove it via a belt from the flywheel.

It was not difficult to adapt existing engines, but there is no record of how many were treated in this way. We do know, however, that the first Burrell to be specially built as a showman's engine was works number 1451 of 1889 and that it went to Jacob Studt of Pontypridd where it carried the enticing name of Jacob Studt's Steam Circus. It created quite a stir and Burrell featured the Studt Circus engine in their 1909 catalogue, together with some impressive photos of steam haulage. One engine was shown hauling Hancock's Great West of England Steam Switchback. The dismantled ride was spread out over four wagons making a total load of 28 tons. It was not only an impressive example of steam haulage but an indication that the fairground itself was becoming ever more complex, relying more and more on steam power.

The showman's engine became a very distinctive machine. The engine had an overall canopy to keep the workings dry, and this was often supported on ornate pillars. The sides of the canopy could be used to advertise the specific ride with which it operated and the whole engine as it made its way from town to town was a mobile advert of the delights in store. Another feature of the engine was the detachable chimney extension that carried the smoke away high above the heads of the crowd, once it was at work at the fairground. Many engines also had detachable small jib cranes. These were versatile machines. Showman's engines are still popular features at many steam fairs, but it is rare that visitors have the opportunity to see exactly what they do. Some years ago, I was asked to write and present a TV documentary for Channel 4 on the Great Dorset Steam Fair and one thing I was really keen to do was to show exactly what these wonderful machines could do. Fortunately, we were able to follow the full story of the work down by a Fowler engine named *Renown*.

The engine was ordered by John Murphy, but production was a little later than expected and was still in a works' blue paint when Murphy arrived to take delivery for the start of the season. He accepted it as it was and blue it remained, with the addition of the caption on the canopy – Murphy's Proud Peacocks. The ride

was a traditional roundabout, but on this occasion many decades later it was not proud Peacocks that arrived at the showground behind the engine, but Harry Lee's Steam Yachts. This ride consists of a pair of swing boats, powered by a separate donkey engine. The undersides of the two boats are decorated, one with the Union Jack and the other with the Stars and Stripes. The idea was to cash in on the huge public interest in the America Cup yacht races. Sir Thomas Lipton, the tea magnate, tried for many years to win the cup, held by America, starting with his yacht *Shamrock* in 1899 and ending with *Shamrock V* in 1930. He never won, but got a specially commissioned cup for 'the best of all losers'. In spite of the patriotic enthusiasm of the public for his efforts, he was not allowed into the Royal Yacht Club until just before his death – a self-made man was not considered quite the right sort of chap to enter such an exclusive club. Today's visitors seem just as happy to ride in the American swing car as in the British.

Having arrived at the ground with its load, *Renown* now added the jib crane to a bracket at the rear of the engine, which could then be used to erect the ride. The first job was to put down the base, after which the great A-frames had to be lifted into the vertical position and accurately located into sockets in the solid

A Fowler engine photographed just as night begins to fall. It was not just the rides that were illuminated; the engine itself is as brilliantly lit as the steam gallopers behind it.

The Fowler engine *Renown* with a very accurate description of the machine itself: 'Plain but Powerful'. The chimney extension, to carry smoke away above the heads of the crowd, can be seen resting on the canopy. At the Dorset Steam Fair this was the engine filmed erecting the ride seen in the next photograph. The crane used in the process can be seen at the rear of the engine.

base board. These were linked by an overhead bar from which the swing boats were suspended. Once that was all secure, the small engine that would drive the boats was wheeled into place, the swing boats suspended and the drive chains attached to the engine. Once everything was set up, the jib was dismantled and cables laid to link the engine's dynamo to the lighting system, ready for nightfall. That was not quite the end of the story as far as I was concerned. The director and I were discussing just how to end the story and as far as I was concerned, the obvious choice seemed to be to do a piece talking to camera on one of the swing boats that had been such an important part of the story we were telling. What I had not realised was that when the boats get going, they seem to swing through 180°, so that you are constantly swooping from a comfortable horizontal to a dizzying vertical and back again – it quite literally takes your breath away. And trying to talk at all was a challenge, let alone trying to sound sensible.

The Steam Yachts with its two swing boats named after the competitors for the Americas Cup; the successful American yacht *Columbia* and the British competitor *Shamrock.* When they are swinging, they display the Stars and Stripes and Union Jack on the bottom of the boats.

But somehow we made it and what it may have lacked in clarity it made up for in atmosphere.

There was one other feature of the ride that had been put in place: a tiny Chippa steam organ with its own animated figure, representing one of the Strauss family, complete with a waving baton. It also had its own small steam engine for power. These organs had become a major attraction at fairs. Before that any music at the fair depended on hiring musicians or using simple mechanical devices, such as the barrel organ. The barrel organs were hand operated by turning a handle. A simple crank operated bellows that provided the compressed air that could be fed into pipes. Each pipe represented a different note, and as the barrel was turned, pins on the outside connected with keys to open valves, determining which pipe got the air and so the note that was played. Most barrel organs carried no more than half a dozen tunes. The fairground organ was altogether more complex.

The basis remained the same – bellows provided air to tuned tubes but the way the keys were operated was very different. Instead of

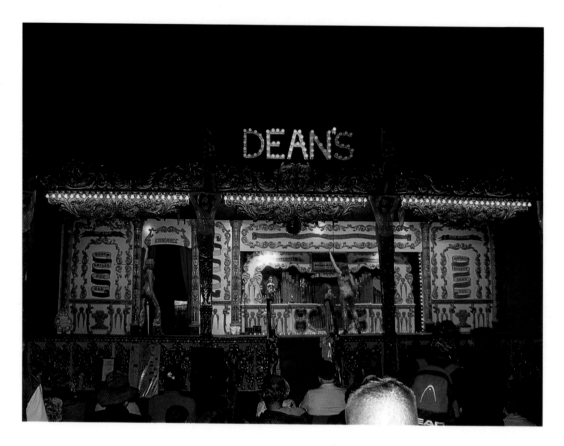

Dean's Bioscope at the Dorset steam fair. It has just about everything up front to attract the customers; the sparkling coloured lights, glamorous dancers and the fairground organ with its animated figures in the centre. Inside the audience watches a variety of old silent films.

spikes on a barrel, the organs got their musical instructions through punched cards. In a large organ, there can be more than 500 pipes, some representing brass instruments such as trumpets, others woodwind and strings. The positioning of the holes decreed which pipes received the air, so determining which 'instruments' will be heard and which notes played, and the length of the holes how long a note should last. With this system, it was possible to play very complex music, and as well as the organ sounds there would also be percussion instruments to provide the basic rhythm. The cards are sewn together into books, which are fed through the machine at a steady rate by a motor. The fairground organ can play as many tunes as there are books available, each tune generally lasting 4 or 5 minutes. The organs not only produce a very distinctive, and to connoisseurs of this music, beautiful and evocative sound, but they are also always highly decorated, with elaborate frames and animated figures.

At the end of the nineteenth century, a new invention brought another exotic attraction to the fairground. In February 1895, the Lumière brothers showed their first moving picture, rather appropriately a short film showing delegates arriving for a photographic conference. These new films attracted immense interest and, in the days before cinemas existed, one of the places they were shown was at fairs in travelling cinemas, known as bioscopes. These were among the most exotic attractions on offer; as well as the one-reelers, there were generally live shows between the films and crowds were drawn in by some of the most elaborate fairground organs ever built. The tradition still lives on. Richard Dean and his son Tom are among the few people still building fairground organs, and they also have their own travelling bioscope show that they take to steam fairs. It is a magnificent affair and, of course, comes complete with an equally splendid organ. But the Deans are very near to completing an even grander fairground organ, and although not quite complete, I can vouch for the fact that already it makes the most fantastically rich sound. It is good to know that the traditions survive.

The Beamish Open Air Museum in Durham is just one of a number of sites that hosts a permanent old style fairground. The steam gallopers are one of the main attractions. As the horses go round and round, they are moved up and down by the vertical poles on which they rest.

One unusual feature of the steam yachts was the need for three separate engines to provide all the power for the swing boats, organ and lighting. Manufacturers began to think about ways to avoid situations like this for complex rides by using the haulage engine itself to power the rides. The solution was to build a turret by extending the hornplates from the firebox. The turret had to be high enough to carry the 'cheese wheel' – the device that provided the rotary motion for the gallopers. The wheel was either driven by a vertical shaft from the crankshaft or even by a small subsidiary engine. Once the base plate for the ride was in place, the traction engine was driven into the centre and the ride built round it. The obvious disadvantage was that it was no longer available to help in the construction process, but some showmen thought it worth the inconvenience. The ride master had all the power under his own control in the centre of the ride.

Various attempts were made to improve on the showman's engine over the years, not all of them very successful. One company took out a patent for a traction engine with a steam organ permanently attached to the front, which might have worked well

At the heart of the Beamish gallopers is this single cylinder steam engine built by Savage.

enough once it reached the fairground but would surely have been a nightmare for anyone on the move. It is doubtful if any of these engines were actually built. Savages built a number of conventional turret engines. Fowlers went one better with their Whirligig engine, which as well as the turret for the ride, had a separate small engine mounted at the side of the smoke box to work an organ.

As rides became more complex, so new demands were made on the traction engines. In 1880, Savages developed a new ride known as the switchback. On the gallopers, the individual horses went up and down, but on this ride, people sat in little carriages that circled on an undulating track. Also known as a scenic railway, a new version appeared in 1910 powered by an electric motor but which still relied on the steam-powered dynamo. The problem was that getting the train of eight cars started from rest required a surge of power, far greater than the simple dynamo could supply. An extra device, the exciter, was added, driven by a belt from the main dynamo. The exciter was often only used at the start of the day's rides; once everything was up and running, the ride was slowed down sufficiently to allow people to get on and off but never brought to a full stop.

Big, exotic rides were popular with the public, and they required more and more power. Manufacturers produced specialist engines for these rides. Burrell built an 8hp engine with an extra wide flywheel for the belt drive, a dynamo producing 29,700 watts and an exciter adding an extra 8,800 watts. Even that was not enough when the designers of rides came up with ever more elaborate ideas. One version had the ride itself, brilliant coloured lights, an organ and, to complete the attraction, a cascade. The latter required a pump to keep the water circulating. It needed two engines to keep the whole thing going, and they worked at the comparatively high boiler pressure of 200psi.

Showmen were always keen to use anything that looked likely to pull in the paying customers. One of the most astute showmen was G.T. Tuby, who realised that a wave of patriotism was engulfing the country during the Boer War. He already had an ornate scenic ride, Tuby's Circular Railway, liberally decorated with gaudy gilt, while the punters waltzed round in gondolas to the accompaniment of organ music. Now he embellished it with pictures of British Generals, the heroes of the day. The war ended and the generals were forgotten and a new craze caught the public imagination, the motor car. Out went the Circular Railway as it was renamed Tuby & Sons 60hp Panhard Motors. Panhard had achieved fame by taking

Fowler Class R Showmans Scenic type Engine with exciter. No. 15658

both first and second places in the Paris-Bordeaux-Paris race of 1895 – but not in a car with anything like 60 horse power under the bonnet. Showmen were never averse to a little exaggeration.

Tuby was a citizen of Doncaster and took an active part in local affairs. As he moved up the political ladder, so the names of his engines were changed to match his status – *Councillor* started things off, to be followed by *Alderman* and eventually *Mayor*. At least he had a sense of humour – the one after that was named *Ex-Mayor*! Steam continued to be a vital part of all big fairs; hauling rides, erecting them, powering them, providing music and lighting the fair at night. The big change came with the arrival of the diesel engine, which could take over all the functions that had once relied on steam, more economically and without the need for constant stoking. That might have been the end of the story, but there was always a glamour attached to the steam engine that the diesel could never match. Today the steam fair is as popular as ever, whether on permanent sites such as the Hollycombe Museum or in travelling fairs that have become annual events in many parts of the country. They do exactly what they have always done: pull in the crowds and provide huge enjoyment to everyone from toddlers to grandparents.

CHAPTER EIGHT

Horseless Carriages for Gentlemen

Restrictive legislation may have limited the development of commercial passenger vehicles on British roads, but that did not stop individuals from building steam carriages for their own use nor did it prevent wealthy patrons ordering them from engineers. Among the pioneers of lightweight steam carriages was a Mr. Boulton of Ashton-under-Lyne, who began building them in 1848 and produced six altogether, though no two seem to have been exactly the same. The one illustrated on p.36 is a rather fragile looking vehicle, with carriage springs to the rear and the small front wheel was also sprung. Steam was provided by the vertical boiler at 60psi. and fed to two cylinders, three inches in diameter with a six inch stroke. The drive from the crankshaft was via a chain to the rear driving axle. Only one wheel was keyed to the drive axle and the other ran loose, so there was no need for any form of compensating gear. It is perhaps rather surprising to find there was no reversing gear; the machine was so light, weighing in at just 17cwt. (0.85 tonnes) that the driver simply stopped and turned it round manually and then set off again. There was a small store of coke and water under the rear seat and it was capable of speeds of around ten miles an hour. It was said that it made long journeys, 'frequently' without any accident. One does wonder exactly how infrequent the actual accidents were. It must have provided a great deal of fun for the family, and Boulton's young son 'ran it about like a tricycle'.

Among the aristocratic patrons for early carriages was the Marquis of Stafford who owned a carriage built in 1858 by Thomas Rickett of the Castle Foundry in Buckingham. It was a three-wheeled vehicle with a chain drive from the crankshaft to the driving axle. It was sufficiently successful to encourage another nobleman, the Earl of Caithness, to order one as well. This was built to a slightly different design. Instead of the chain drive it had spur gearing. It had two cylinders and two sets of gears, giving speeds of 10 and 4mph, and the low gear was probably essential for a vehicle that was meant to spend its working life trundling up and down hills in the Scottish Highlands. It carried up to three passengers, who were probably

Although the machine looks rather flimsy and the front wheel quite spindly, this carriage by L. W. Boulton of Ashton-under-Lyne was reportedly so easy to handle that the inventor's small son could manage it. Perhaps he is one of the boys taking a ride at the back.

glad of the extra comfort provided by good springing. Carriages such as these were generally one-offs and very few have survived to the present day. One which has survived, though it has seen a few alterations over the years, is the Grenville steam carriage.

The carriage was the brainchild of Robert Neville Grenville who had studied mechanical engineering at the South Devon railway workshops at Newton Abbot. He built it in his spare time over a period of some 15 years with the help of a fellow student at Newton Abbot, George Jackson Churchward. The latter was to become a hugely influential designer of locomotives as Chief Mechanical Engineer for the Great Western Railway, and he is best known for the fact that it was during his time as chief engineer that Swindon works turned out *City of Truro*, the first locomotive to reach a speed of a hundred miles per hour. The engine he helped Grenville build as a student was considerably more modest, though it was recorded as comfortably reaching speeds of 20mph on the flat. The little machine does, however, show the marks of its origins with a pair of young railway engineers, especially in the chassis and the wheels and it is possible some of it was actually constructed at the G.W.R. works at Swindon.

The vehicle was supplied with a vertical boiler probably built by Shand Mason & Co. who at the time were supplying similar boilers for pumps on horse-drawn fire engines. It was originally planned with a single cylinder but later acquired two. It was possible to work it with a crew of one. The driver at the front would have control over the throttle and cut off levers and would also steer by means of a tiller attached to the single front wheel. In practice, it is much easier to handle with a crew of two at the front. The firebox is at the rear, where the fireman would perch. In these early steam vehicles, while wealthy owners might be happy to have the controls under their own hands, they preferred to leave the dirty business of shovelling coal to someone else. In English this would be a fireman, but was usually given the French equivalent name – chauffeur, a name that stuck long after anyone stopped using coal-fired carriages.

It is not altogether clear just when the vehicle was first run but it is generally given a date of around 1880. Shand Mason fitted a replacement boiler to the same design in 1930 and the carriage eventually found a home in the Bristol Industrial Museum. When that museum closed, to be replaced by the present M-Shed on the same site, Bristol decided, inexplicably, that it had no place for this unique survivor. Fortunately it has a new and very appropriate home at the National Motor Museum in Beaulieu. To find another example that has survived from this period one has to travel across the Atlantic, where Dudgeon's steam carriage is on show in the Smithsonian Collection.

Richard Dudgeon was born in the Scottish Highlands in 1819, but his father went to America and eventually brought the whole family over to join him. They settled at first in New Hartford, now part of Utica. The boy showed an early aptitude for mechanical engineering and, after his apprenticeship, he got a job at the Allaire Iron works in New York. This was a good choice as they were a famously innovative company and the owner had an important connection with the world of steam: he had cast some of the parts for Robert Fulton's famous steamboat *Clermont.* Dudgeon married in 1848 and began his own machine shop at Willett Street, New York. His fortune was assured when in 1851 he designed a 'portable hydraulic press' or as we would now call it a hydraulic jack.

Various liquids could be used, and in harsh winter conditions, when water would freeze, the manufacturers recommended using whiskey. In America it soon became popularly known as the whiskey jack. The business prospered – indeed the company still exists and still makes hydraulic machinery.

Dudgeon decided to build a steam carriage in 1853, largely, he wrote, 'to end the fearful horse murder and numerous other ills inseparable from their use'. He drove it on the streets of New York around his home and works. It incurred the wrath of the authorities, in particular Daniel Tieman, the Mayor of New York. He restricted the use of the carriage to a single street on the old familiar grounds that it would frighten the horses, which is ironic given that Dudgeon was trying to preserve horses from misuse. In 1858 his steam carriage and examples of hydraulic presses were on display at an exhibition at New York's Crystal Palace, America's version of the famous London exhibition hall. On 5 October fire broke out

The Grenville steam carriage is one of the very few of its type to survive into the present day. Here it is being given an outing by members of staff of the former Bristol Industrial Museum. The carriage now has a new home at the National Motor Museum.

and the whole building and its contents, including the Dudgeon carriage, were destroyed. In 1866 he built a second carriage that is the one now preserved at the Smithsonian. When he advertised the fact that he was able to manufacture steam carriages in his 1870 catalogue, he was still smarting over the original banning:

'If anyone makes a good, manageable steam carriage at his own cost and goes everywhere interfering with no one, have it understood that if one tailor says his horse doesn't like it, and shook his head at it, command the steam carriage man never to take it out his door again. That is what old Tieman did to my first.'

The carriage had many of the characteristics of railway locomotives, which is not perhaps surprising given that much of the work was carried out at the Rogers Locomotive Works. It had a horizontal boiler, with the firebox at one end and the chimney at the other. Two cylinders at the front had connecting rods to the rear wheels and the driver and steerer were at the rear of the vehicle, just like the footplate crew of a railway locomotive. An unusual feature for this time was that the steam was superheated. The wheels were made of cedar wood in sections, held together by iron tyres. The drive was managed through a screw and swivel nut to the front axle. Given that the steerer was at the back of the vehicle, this must have made the task quite difficult. Two long water tanks were arranged at either side of the carriage and covered with padded cushions to create the passenger seats. The boiler was covered with coconut matting that provided a foot rest, which must have been cosily warm on winter excursions. The engine ran on coal and was said to bowl along at a very respectable 25-30mph. In spite of this impressive performance there seems to have been little enthusiasm for this form of transport, and very few if any orders were received from customers. The engine remained in the family until the 1940s, when it was sold to a pair of antique dealers, who eventually presented it to the Smithsonian.

Dudgeon was not the only American to work on steam cars. Stephen Roper had worked quietly away at developing steam carriages on his own from 1859, but only told the world at large about his experiments when he wrote to *The Scientific American* in 1863. He began very modestly with a little vehicle of just 2 horse power that moved at a slow walking pace. He went on to develop his ideas, building a total of ten vehicles over a twenty-five-year period.

The Dudgeon carriage built in America, seen here with a motley array of passengers. This version was built in 1886, following a fire in New York's Crystal Palace that destroyed the original. It is now preserved at the Smithsonian in Washington DC.

Francis Curtis was superintendent of the gas works at Newburyport, Mass. who began by working on a steam powered fire engine in 1861. The following year he built a carriage and reading the details it sounds quite impressive. With a boiler working at 40-45psi. it managed speeds of 25mph. But it was a tiny machine, with just a single seat for the operator. It had to be stopped at regular intervals to take on water and the longest run it ever recorded was only 9½ minutes. In spite of its limitations, Curtis got an order for a machine, and the customer agreed a price of $1000 to be paid in instalments. The instalments, however, failed to appear and Curtis grabbed the machine back again – the first car repossession that has ever been recorded. His troubles did not end there, however, as a neighbour not only objected to his appearing on the local roads but managed to acquire a warrant for his arrest. The constabulary duly arrived, and in what must have been like a scene from a Keystone Cops movie, Curtis set off in his steamer, pursued by puffing policemen on foot. The early days of steam on the road in America were certainly not without incident.

One of the most curious – and certainly one of the most elaborate – carriages was the work of a British engineer, H. Percy Holt. Outwardly, it looked very little different from other light road vehicles, a three-wheeled carriage with a pair of 4ft 6 in drive wheels and a 2ft 6in front wheel for steering. It was fitted with a Field boiler that hung off the back of the iron frame that worked at a pressure of 250psi. The big difference was in the engine, or to be

more precise, engines. For this carriage was fitted with two engines, each with two identical cylinders and each driving independent crankshafts. The exhaust steam was passed into a cast iron box, placed above the firebox, allowing the steam to be superheated. Because each engine could be operated independently, the speed of each drive wheel could be adjusted to make cornering easier and the reversing gear could be used as a brake. The cylinders themselves were set at an angle. Fuel could be saved once the machine was set on a good level stretch of road, by turning off the steam to one of the pair of engines. It was said to be able to take a 1 in 14 incline at 7mph. and if run on the flat on a good road was able to reach 20mph. Although the machine weighed a modest 1.5 tonnes it was able to carry as many as eight passengers and was, according to a contemporary account, 'much more powerful than will be required for the moderate speeds of the future'. As we shall see in the next chapter, the author of those words could not have foreseen what the next decades would bring about in the way of progress.

J. G. Inshaw's 1881 carriage from the photograph he supplied to *The Engineer* magazine in 1893. It was a sophisticated machine, with three gears but remained a one off.

Leonard Todd's steam carriage had a sporty appearance and, unlike most of the others, had a canopy offering some protection from the weather. The steam cylinders were boxed in and the drive was taken to the rear wheels via a gut rope. The illustration appeared in *The Engineer* 7th February 1896.

Of all the carriages developed at this time, the one that seemed to offer the best option as a sporty, light carriage was the two-seater designed by Leonard Todd. Like the Holt, it had two separate engines, but this time only one cylinder per engine and quite small, just 2½ in diameter and 4 in stroke. The cylinders were set either side of the vertical boiler, near the front of the vehicle, and drive was taken from grooved pulleys on the crankshaft via gut cords to the rear wheels. There was no reversing gear but it was fitted with brakes to the rear wheels operated by a foot pedal. It was extremely light and very well sprung and ran so smoothly and economically that the engineer guaranteed it could cover a hundred miles in ten hours. The engine was worked by the man in the right hand seat being responsible for driving, steering and braking, while the other did the firing. There was a great deal of interest in this sporty little machine, but ultimately no more were built, largely because of the restrictions laid down by law in the infamous Road Locomotives Act.

The point was emphasised by J. G. Inshaw, who wrote an article for *The Engineer* of 1 November 1881 about his own machine that is worth quoting at some length:

'I have much pleasure in handing you a photograph of an experimental steam carriage built by me in 1881: the carriage was well known in Birmingham and district, and its working was most satisfactory. The only reason I had for discontinuing my experiments was in consequence of the law prohibiting the use of steam-propelled carriages on the common road, although the carriage made no more noise than an ordinary vehicle, and the exhaust steam being entirely condensed, there was nothing against steam, which I am very much in favour of now and intend making another carriage as soon as the law has been repealed, which I hope will happen very soon.

'I have much pleasure in giving you a few particulars of this carriage. The boiler was almost entirely composed of steel tubes, and would generate steam in about twenty minutes to a pressure of 180 lbs. to 200 lbs, per square inch, finding steam for two cylinders, 4-in bore, 8-in stroke. There were three different speeds for hill climbing etc. There was also double driving gear, and, in fact, all the necessary contrivances were to be found in this machine. The steering was very satisfactory and quite easy to manage.

'When loaded with ten passengers, fuel and water, the carriage weighed 35 cwt,. and the speed on a good road averaged from eight to twelve miles per hour. The steerer had entire control over the carriage; in fact, far more than a coachman over a pair of horses, and during the whole of my experiments, which lasted for several years, I never had the slightest accident of any kind.'

This was clearly a sophisticated machine but it seems that, thwarted by Parliament, Inshaw never developed his invention.

The latter part of the nineteenth century saw a number of experiments with light carriages, mainly in Britain and America. There was an experimental vehicle made by a Mr. Jochumsen of Denmark but the boiler proved too small for it to run efficiently and in spite of a number of attempts to improve matters, it never took to the road. Others described in this chapter were capable of further development had the circumstances of the time allowed. But there was always something of a problem in attracting large numbers of customers. It was all very well for the wealthy to send out a man to prepare the engine and raise steam perhaps twenty minutes or half an hour before a journey could start, but for an ordinary individual who did not enjoy the luxury of employing a chauffeur the delay would have been intensely irritating. There was the added disadvantage that, once under way, a second pair of hands was always necessary to keep the fire going while the owner had the more enjoyable job of driving the engine. This would always be the case as long as the boiler had to be fed by coal or coke or even wood. All that was about to change.

CHAPTER NINE

The Steam Car Comes of Age

The late nineteenth century saw the start of a revolution in land transport that had its beginnings far earlier. The steam engine could be described as an external combustion engine in that the fire is used to turn water into steam and it is the steam that provides the power. The alternative is the internal combustion engine; the sort we have in a modern motor car, but its origins date back to the seventeenth century when Christiaan Huygens devised his 'gunpowder engine'. It had the usual arrangement of a piston in a tightly fitting cylinder. When gunpowder was added below the piston and lit, the expanding gases from the explosion forced the piston up the cylinder. At the top of the stroke, holes were uncovered that allowed the gases to escape, after which air pressure forced the piston back down again. It was not, however, a very practical machine as no one worked out how to keep feeding in the gunpowder. It was only in the nineteenth century that the basic idea was adapted to create a useful engine. The development of the internal combustion engine had a profound effect on steam road vehicles, offering new possibilities but also dangerous competition. It did not seem so at first.

The first real breakthrough was made in 1859 by the Frenchman Étienne Lenoir who designed an engine in which the explosive force was provided by a mixture of gas and air, ignited by an electric spark. It proved too expensive to run, costing a great deal more than the equivalent steam engine. The next stage of development was the work of another French engineer, Alphonse Beau de Rochas. He proposed a cycle of events based on a horizontal engine. It began when the piston was moving towards the crankshaft and the gas-air mixture was drawn into the cylinder. On the second stroke, the gas was compressed and at dead centre, the gas was ignited, driving the piston for the third stroke. On the final stroke, the burnt gases were exhausted from the cylinder. This is the four-stroke cycle – injection, compression, ignition, exhaust. He patented the idea, but never developed it and the patent lapsed. In 1878, the German engineer Nikolaus Otto developed the same idea – it is not clear whether or not he had heard of the Beau de Rochas - but the 4-stroke cycle became known as the Otto cycle.

Léon Serpollet's coal-fired steam tricycle of 1887; the power plant is entirely contained within the rear driving wheels. With the exhaust passing up the chimney just behind the driver's back, it must have been uncomfortably warm.

He was a practical engineer who realised that he could use coal gas as a fuel and that this was a commercially viable system. Within a few years over 30,000 Otto gas engines, manufactured by Otto & Langen, were at work all round the world. There were obvious advantages to the new engines, not least the fact that they could be worked from a town gas supply and no one had to be paid to keep a furnace stoked to provide the power. But that also meant that they were strictly limited to wherever the gas was supplied – they were not at this stage of any value to the world of transport. No one seriously considered the idea of taking a large reservoir of methane gas along to keep a vehicle moving. But once the idea of the internal combustion engine had been well and truly established and its advantages appreciated, it was only a matter of time before new ways of using it would be found. What was needed was an easily portable fuel source.

Various engineers began developing engines run on oil, of whom the best known is Rudolf Diesel, whose name, of course, became all but synonymous with engines burning heavy oil. But we are still in the age of stationary engines; it was to be another German, Gottleib Daimler, who was to start a new transport revolution. Instead of being based on diesel oil, his version used lighter petroleum, which was easily vaporised. To produce the right petrol-air mixture, he invented the carburettor in 1885. His engine was light and high speed, and that same year he installed an engine in a bicycle; the world's first commercially successful oil-fired motorbike. It was not long before men such as Karl Benz were developing the petrol engine for use in a motor car. The petrol-engine car became an almost immediate success and might well have marked the end of steam on the road. But the steam engineers also realised that it offered them

The Serpollet phaeton of 1891 developed out of the tricycle. This illustration from *The Engineer* of the time shows the mechanical arrangement, with the connecting rod from the piston ending in gears that take the chain drive back to the rear wheels. Coke was used as the fuel and 150lb was stored in panniers. With an average consumption of 3lb a mile this should have been enough for 50 miles of non-stop travel, but unfortunately water consumption was much higher at 15lb a mile.

THE SERPOLLET STEAM PHÆTON, 1891

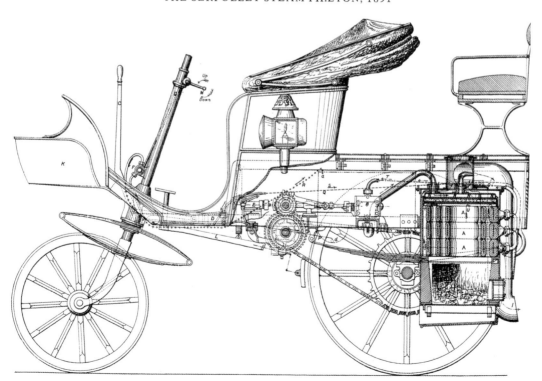

a new opportunity. One of the disadvantages of existing steam vehicles was the need to employ a chauffeur whose job it was to stoke up the fire. He would no longer be needed if one was able to use oil or petrol as the fuel to raise steam in the boiler. A new generation of steam vehicles was about to emerge. From now on a chauffeur would only be needed to drive the cars of the rich who preferred not to do the task themselves. The advent of the motor car had another immediate advantage for the steam men. It brought into being a new and powerful lobby to argue against the speed restrictions then in force. It was their influence as much as anything that led to the repeal of the Red Flag Act and the raising of speed limits, as helpful to steam vehicle owners as it was to motorists.

One of the first engineers to take advantage of the new technology was Léon Serpollet. The French industrialist established a factory in Paris – now the site of the Parc Léon Serpollet where a statue to the inventor has been erected. He was interested in producing lightweight vehicles. His first effort in 1887 was a coal-fired steam tricycle, with the engine fitted between the two rear driving wheels. It can hardly have been a very practical device, as the rider would have had to get off every time the fire needed replenishing. This, however, was of only minor importance and it set him thinking about ways in which the steam carriage could be made more effective, in particular, how to raise steam more quickly and more efficiently. The answer he came up with in 1889 was the flash boiler.

The boiler consists of flattened steel tubes, arranged in coils, with a small gap of around 10mm between the tubes. The feed water is fed into the bottom of the coils, where it is almost instantly turned into steam, which, as it travels up the coils, becomes superheated. In tests carried out on one of the Serpollet vehicles it was found that although the steam pressure was not excessive at around 250psi, it left the boiler at over 1000°F, nearly three times as high as that from a conventional boiler at the same pressure. The Serpollet vehicles were still using solid fuels, usually coke. Nevertheless, they were extremely successful and Serpollet went into partnership with a wealthy American, Frank Gardner, to form Gardner-Serpollet. It was in one of their vehicles, known as the 'Easter Egg' that Serpollet established a world land speed record in 1902, driving his car on a 1 kilometre course along the Boulevard des Anglais in Nice at a speed of 120 km per hour (74.5mph).

Serpollet's contribution to vehicle and boiler development was immense but because it used fuels such as coke, it still required someone to keep stoking the fire. It did, however, possess huge advantages, notably in raising steam almost instantaneously and in being much lighter than earlier steam carriages. Now engineers began to take the next step, which was to start using paraffin as a fuel instead of coal and coke. The development of oil fields in the middle of the nineteenth century had largely rested on a demand for kerosene for oil lamps. This was widely available, while petrol was still comparatively scarce. In the early twentieth century, many experts felt that steam had a much better future than did the newly developed petrol driven cars. It is interesting to see what partisans thought of the new-fangled machines that had arrived on the road. William Fletcher, writing in 1906, listed all the disadvantages he could think of that affected the newcomer and set those against the advantages of steam.

The Stanley twins photographed around September 1897 in one of the very earliest versions of their steam car. Although the engine may have been up to date, the carriage work is a simple adaptation of a small horse-drawn buggy.

Petrol Engine	Steam Engine
Derives its motion from a gas explosion, which is momentary, non-elastic – resembling the blow of a hammer	Derives it motion from a steady and expansive pressure of the steam which is maintained to the end of the stroke
The strength of the explosion cannot be increased	The pressure can be doubled at will
Is noisy, causes violent vibration, and exhausts offensive fumes	Is practically silent and free from vibration
Has to be started by hand, frequently resulting in injury to the starter from backfiring, and always necessitating considerable exertion and caution	After lighting the burner, can be started immediately
Is always difficult to reverse	Is instantly self-reversing
Requires knowledge and experience in manipulating the numerous admissions of gas, air, mixture, etc.	Only requires the steam turned on or off
Requires a battery, coil, and a complicated system of electrical sparking to ignite the gas	Requires no ignition
Necessitates the use of a highly inflammable and dangerous spirit, a spark only being sufficient to cause explosion	American paraffin is used as fuel
Petrol can only be obtained at places where it is specially kept	Paraffin can be obtained anywhere.
Petrol costs from 1s to 1s. 6d a gallon	Paraffin costs from 5d to 8d a gallon
Requires circulating water to prevent it from becoming red hot	Does not heat beyond the temperature of the steam
Is liable to refuse to work from an infinitude of causes requiring expert knowledge to locate	Should troubles occur, are easily located

Some of the objections to the motor car now seem rather quaint – especially the 'exorbitant' price of petrol – but others are still valid. Anyone who has had to use a starting handle will know of the perils involved and exhaust fumes are as troublesome now as they were a century ago. And, as we shall see shortly, running a steam car was not quite as simple as Fletcher suggests. But many were convinced that there was quite enough in favour of steam for it to have a long and successful future and to keep the opposition at bay.

The last years of the nineteenth century saw many experiments with comparatively light carriages, with a variety of different boilers and means of heating. One early pioneer was W. H. Brown of Devizes, whose carriage was powered by a two-cylinder compound engine, working at 200psi. This carriage was fitted with an oil burner from the start and used one of Brown's own design. It was able to carry enough fuel for a trip of 70 to 100 miles on 'level roads', but had to stop every twenty-five miles to take on water. But as the maximum speed was 12mph, it was good for at least a couple of hours travelling. This, however, was simply a carriage made for the owner and there was never any attempt to put it into production.

Some engineers remained wedded to coke as a fuel, but others were soon using petrol or paraffin. Many were one offs, which Fletcher thought was the best way forward. One such vehicle was an open steam carriage devised by a Mr. Phillipson, working with the engineering firm of Toward in Newcastle. It was described as being capable of speeds 'in excess of anything that will be permitted by Government regulations', though given the regulations then in force that was not saying a great deal. It was said to be free from vibration and could comfortably go up hills as steep as 1 in 9. It had a different sort of flash boiler, with coiled steel tubes inside. It was an early example of a carriage that could be fuelled by either coke or petrol, though on the whole, rather surprisingly, they recommended the former. An interesting point is that the designers opted for solid rubber tyres rather than pneumatic. They claimed that the latter were too apt to puncture, which might well have been true given the nature of the roads at that time. It was sufficiently successful to be put into production and a small number were constructed, mainly sold in the north of England. Fletcher was particularly keen on this model and wrote of the designers' ability to overcome problems, such as providing power for a light vehicle:

'The great point for congratulation is the fact that the difficulty has been overcome by private enterprise, by two old fashioned firms of coachbuilders and engineers working in harmony, and conclusively proving that more good will be done in this way than by motor companies, promoted by men with no practical knowledge either of engineering or coachmaking.'

Fletcher was wrong; the future lay now with large manufacturers. And no one produced more steam cars in the early years than Stanley. The Stanley steamer became so popular that it even made it into a popular song, featured in the 1948 movie *Summer Holiday*, starring Mickey Rooney and Gloria de Haven. Here's the first verse:

'Get your veil and get your duster,
Get the yen for goggles when the wind's a guster
Keep your Hubbard gown
Firmly belted down
When you're out in your Stanley Steamer.
In a gale we never fluster,
'Cause we're told we get that old familiar lustre
If you're dressed in style
Ev'ry one will smile
When you're out in your Stanley Steamer.
Honk, honk!
Honk, honk, honk!
The donkey used to have his charm;
But he's looking at us with alarm,
For it looks like he's back to the farm.
But if you fail with your combustor,
Then your speed is gonna need a new adjuster;
And you must be just,
Just the one we trust;
Or we won't step inside
No, we won't take the ride
That you plan in your Stanley Steamer,
That you plan in your Stanley Steamer
In your Stanley Steamer automobile.'

I shall spare the reader any more of the lyrics, but anyone interested to hear it can find a recording online, sung by Jo Stafford. And there was no resisting including a still from the film, with the featured 1910 model. But now it is time to go back to the start of the Stanley story.

Freelan Oscar and Francis Edgar Stanley were identical twins born in Maine in 1849. They showed an entrepreneurial spirit from

Freelan and Flora Stanley on the summit of Mount Washington in 1899. The road was only 7.6 miles long, but it had a vertical rise of 4,725 feet and the flimsy looking car managed the task in 2 hours 10 minutes.

an early age; when just ten years old they set up a little business refining and selling maple sugar. Many small boys have dreamed up schemes to make extra pocket money but very few would have used it to buy a book on arithmetic and then steadily work through every equation in the book. Freelan showed a very practical bent and having been taught by his uncle how to make violins, continued making them throughout his life. These were not merely amateur efforts and are highly prized instruments. Both brothers went on to further education, but Francis dropped out to take up a career as a portrait artist. Freelan continued with his education, eventually joining Bowdoin College, New Brunswick. He never graduated, not because of any lack of ability, but due to a system introduced by the new president of the college, Joshua Chamberlain, who brought in compulsory military drill for all students. Many objected and tried to get the decision reversed. They failed, but most of the protestors accepted the failure. Stanley did not and was expelled for standing by his principles. Both brothers had shown independent spirits in their different ways.

For a time, they followed different paths. Freelan became headmaster of a school in Maine but when he was struck by tuberculosis, which he was lucky to survive, he decided for a change in life style. He set up the Stanley Practical Drawing Set factory, which was thriving until it was devastated by fire in 1882. Meanwhile his brother had taken up photography, and following the fire he suggested they got together to develop a new type

A **1911** Stanley. By this date the steam car had taken on an appearance very similar to that of contemporary motor cars, such as the Model T Ford. There is nothing much to indicate that it is powered by steam, unless one happens to be near it when running; the steam car was very quiet compared with the automobiles.

of photographic plate. Dry plate photography had first been developed in Britain in 1871 and had been improved over the next decade, but most photographers still used the wet plate process. The Stanleys decided to establish a factory to manufacture the new plates and they were hugely successful. By 1890 they had moved to Newton, Massachusetts, were very wealthy and were soon looking for new avenues to explore. It was Francis who first showed an interest in automobiles and he looked at the three possible means of power: electricity, internal combustion and steam. He decided that the future lay with steam and began building his first steam car, which was taken to the Boston Auto Show in 1898. It attracted a huge amount of interest and they began a new business, the Stanley Motor Carriage Company, building vehicles to order.

In 1899, John Brisben Walker, a successful magazine publisher, offered to buy the business. The Stanley brothers were unwilling to sell, but were businessmen first and foremost, so they set what they thought was an unrealistically high price. That way they won either way; they kept their own business or made a very high profit. The price they set was $250,000 - $7.3 million at today's prices. To their astonishment, Walker agreed, but to raise the finance he had to go into partnership with Amzi L. Barber, known as the Asphalt King, as he had made a fortune from having a near monopoly in installing pavements of that material. The Stanley twins continued

By **1916,** when this model was produced, the Stanley Company was nearing the end of its life in control of the two brothers. It would never really recover and cars such as this represent its finest achievement.

as advisers, Francis concentrating on manufacturing and Freelan on marketing. The new car was known as the Stanley Locomobile and Freelan showed himself to be an imaginative promoter. His most famous exploit was to drive the new vehicle with his wife Flora as passenger up the Mount Washington Carriage Road. This route, opened in 1861, climbs to the 6145ft summit of the mountain with an average gradient of 11.7 per cent. It was quite an adventure. 'We went on, and up, up, still up, ', wrote Flora Stanley, 'the continuous climbing being varied only by a steepness so excessive that we felt a sickening anxiety least each brilliant dash should be our last'. There was a greater anxiety, once they had reached the summit. They had to go back down in a vehicle, with only a hand brake fitted, which meant that they had to rely on using the engine to stop themselves careering out of control. Mrs. Stanley made light of it. 'This proved as easy as falling off a log. We reversed the engine, played the brake like an organ pedal, just held on and let the thing spin.' Even today, the drive is considered quite a test, and motorists who pay the toll to use the route get a bumper sticker to announce they have achieved it. It must have been extraordinary over a century ago.

The partnership between Walker and Barber was short lived; Barber formed a new company, the Mobile Company of America, while Walker's Locomobile company was to abandon steam in favour of the internal combustion engine. The Stanley brothers decided to start up again on their own. Walker still had their original patents, but they had already decided that it was time to introduce a new, improved model of steam car and in 1901 production restarted under their original name. One of their first customers was George Eastman, a name famous in photography as the founder of Kodak. He not only bought a car from them, but also acquired the rights to their dry plate system. Now the brothers concentrated entirely on steam cars, and achieved quite remarkable results. In 1906, with Fred Marriott at the wheel, the Stanley *Rocket Racer* broke the world land speed record at Daytona Beach in Florida, reaching a speed of 127.7mph. They tried to improve on that the following year, but the car crashed and became a total wreck. Marriott survived, but the Stanleys abandoned racing and concentrated on producing cars for the general public. They were not prolific, limiting output to a thousand vehicles per year.

One of their aims was to produce comparatively light cars. Early versions had all wooden bodywork, but the chief saving was in the boiler itself. Most steam boilers got their strength by being constructed of heavy metal plates. The Stanley boilers were very different. The outer cylindrical casing was made of thin metal, usually copper, but was wound round with three layers of strong piano wire. They were conventional firetube boilers, with anything from 500 to 1000 tubes. They were nominally rated as producing steam up to 600psi, but were tested to twice that pressure in the factory. Exploding boilers were a rarity in Stanley steamers. The outer drums varied in size over the years from 14in to 30in diameter and from 14in to 18in in height. The cars themselves were rated by horsepower, as 10, 20 and 30hp, but were capable of far greater power over short periods.

In the 1902 model, the boiler was situated in the rear of the vehicle, so that the driver sat more or less on top of it, which was not very comfortable – and sometimes dangerous, as it was not unknown for flames to shoot upwards from the burner. By 1904, they had changed the boiler position to the front, where it remained for the rest of the production period. The heating arrangement in a Stanley is not straightforward. The fire first heats the fuel that is then passed through a narrow hole and mixed with air, before being ignited to heat the water.

Fletcher had noted in his comparison between petrol and steam engine, that starting the petrol engine required 'exertion and

A still from the film *Summer Holiday*, showing Mickey Rooney at the wheel of a 1910 Stanley. This has the typical rounded front that earned it the name 'coffin nose'.

caution', while of the steam engine he simply wrote that the steam engine 'after lighting the burner can be started immediately'. This might suggest that all the owner had to do was apply a match and away he went, rather as one might light a gas stove. It was certainly not that simple and if it did not require all that much exertion, it certainly required a good deal of caution. Richard J. Evans in his book *Steam Cars* gave a very thorough account of exactly what was required before you could drive off.

The first thing to do would be to make sure there was water not only in the water tank, but also in the boiler itself; if the latter was empty, the hand pump had to be used, so the process was not necessarily free of any exertion. That is all fairly straightforward, but lighting the burner was a complex and potentially hazardous business. Before you can even think of starting the burner you have to vapourise the fuel for the pilot light. This involves heating up all the associated pipe work, by pushing the nozzle of a blowlamp into a special aperture in the pilot vapouriser, and holding it there for at least a quarter of an hour until everything has been warmed up to the right temperature. The blowlamp can then be removed and the pilot valve opened. In theory, the pilot flame should now light – but theory and practice do not always coincide. If the jet has not been cleared properly, instead of the flame appearing, a jet of fuel will run out, onto the engine and the floor. As Evans wryly notes, the 'the natural reaction is to panic, pull out the blowlamp and set the whole thing on fire'. He adds, scarcely reassuringly, that the fire should go out without destroying the car. The next step is to close off the valve, clean up any remaining spilled oil, clear the blockage and start again.

Once the pilot light is working, the blowlamp has to be kept in place for a little longer to let the burner casing heat up. The pressure in the main fuel feed has to be brought up, again by hand, and now the valve to the main burner can be opened. Again, if everything is not hot enough, unlit fuel will escape with equally interesting results and, as with the pilot light, blockages have to be cleared and the process repeated. At this stage, the pilot light

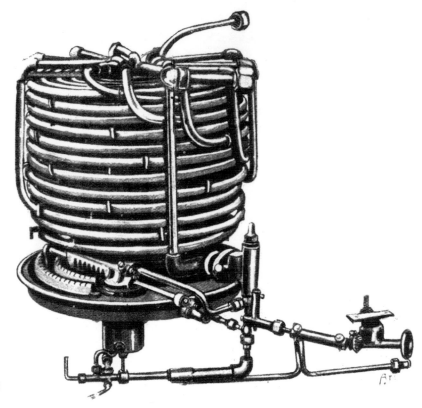

The White steam generator; unlike conventional boilers, the source of heat is below the coils but the water is always injected at the top and stays there under pressure, with steam leaving at the bottom of the coils

will invariably have gone out again and have to be relit, this time with an alarmingly loud bang. Once the burner is lit, just a few more seconds are needed to let steam into the cylinder and at last the car can move off. Experienced drivers will probably manage the different operations without fires, explosions or any other catastrophe, but reading accounts such as this it is hard to agree with the notion that starting an early steam car was a simple matter. Fortunately, as technology advanced, the arrival of electric ignition and flash boilers made the whole job simple and safe. Originally the steam leaving the engine was simply allowed to blow away into the open air, but in later models it was condensed, providing a supply of feed water.

The engine was always a simple two-cylinder design, with slide valves and a Stephenson linkage. Initially the drive was transmitted, as with most road vehicles of this period, by means of a chain to the drive wheels. However, when the Stanleys set out on their own for the second time, this arrangement infringed the patent they had earlier sold to Walker. This turned out to be a blessing, for the answer they came up with was a great improvement. They set the engine directly above the rear driving axle and connected to it; this got rid of all the problems associated with chain drive – tensioning and aligning the chain, keeping it lubricated and clearing out dirt and pebbles to prevent wear and tear. They were so pleased with the new arrangement, that they put it at the head of their adverts. 'Power – Correctly generated, correctly controlled, correctly applied to the rear axle.' The gear ratio between the crankshaft and the differential gear was 1.5:1.

The driver of a Stanley was faced with far more devices than would be found on most modern cars, because of the variety of different functions. To start the engine, the Stanley takes advantage of the fact that the pilot runs on an easily ignited fuel, while the main burner runs on kerosene, which is far more difficult to light. So there has to be a device to shoot pilot fuel into the main burner to start the process. The flow of kerosene is controlled by a valve that has to be closed manually when the vehicle stops. The pilot light retains boiler pressure, until restart time arrives, when the valve is reopened. The actual flow of steam to the engine is controlled by a hand throttle, but the cut-off point can be altered using a foot pedal. With the pedal released, steam is admitted for 80 per cent of the engine stroke, giving maximum power. For ordinary running, the pedal is depressed and hooked into place, so that admission is only happening during 20 per cent of the stroke. Basically, it is doing the same job as the reversing lever on a traction engine but in discreet jumps not as a continuous movement. When fully depressed, the engine is put into reverse. A second pedal operated the brakes on the rear wheel, which was generally regarded as inefficient when moving forward and virtually useless when the vehicle was in reverse. A lever can be used in emergency to pump more water for the boiler. The fuel pump works when the car is moving but fuel has to be pumped by hand during the start-up period.

As well as the controls, there are a number of gauges, so that the driver can keep a check on water levels in the boiler, steam pressure in the boiler and the usual instruments – speedometer and odometer. There was also an unusual device known as the 'winker'. Squirts of oil are delivered regularly to the moving parts, and the winker glass, shows them passing – alternating, dark, white, dark, white – hence the name. The table comparing the advantages of steam over internal combustion, as well as mentioning ease of starting also listed the benefits of steam as including the ease of operation. The author had not perhaps driven a Stanley, though it is not really as difficult as the above description might suggest. A Stanley owner pointed out that, once started, a Stanley was easier to drive than a modern car, with very little to do except manage the hand throttle and steer. It could be started with ease on a slope as little as 1 in 4 and could cruise comfortably at speeds of between 45 and 50mph.

In 1917, the brothers decided it was time to retire and sold the company. With a certain tragic irony, Francis was killed in a road accident shortly afterwards. Freelan lived on until 1940. Sadly, the company stagnated under its new owners; the best days of the Stanley steamer were ended. Other manufacturers, however, continued to make advances and one company that took a very different of boiler design was White.

Thomas H. White was a highly successful manufacturer of sewing machines, who started his business in Massachusetts after the American Civil War and then opened a new factory in Cleveland. It was here that he decided to buy one of the new Locomobiles but was unimpressed with the performance of the boiler. His son Rollin White set about designing an alternative version – technically not a boiler at all. The steam generator consisted of a series of helical coils placed one above the other, with a burner at the bottom. Water was pumped in at the top and the force of the

pump kept it in the upper coils. The heat from the burner turned it into steam, which passed out of the bottom of the system into the engine. Unlike a conventional boiler, there was no need to keep a check on water levels, so no water gauge was required.

In 1900 four cars were built to a very basic design. They were open buggies, with tiller steering and chain drive from a two-cylinder engine placed under the floorboards. The following year production rose to 193 and the same year four White cars took part in an endurance run at Buffalo; all four were awarded first class certificates. Improvements were gradually made. A condenser was added for the exhaust steam and the chain drive was replaced by shaft drive. The engine was moved to the front of the vehicle, under a distinctively curved hood. The vehicles were starting to look like cars, not horseless carriages.

The White machine got a huge publicity boost when they decided to build a racing car in the winter of 1904/5. It was officially known as the 'White Flyer', but was soon popularly known as 'Whistling Billy', from the noise the burners made when it was travelling at speed. The car had a 20hp compound engine, with Stephenson linkage to slide vales. The latter proved inadequate to deal with the high pressure, which for racing was an impressive 800psi, so they were replaced by piston valves that proved so successful that they

A handsome White car. The photograph is undated, but is a very rare example for this period in that it shows a woman at the controls and not even a hint that there should be a man on hand to explain things.

were incorporated into all later White steam cars. The car raced all over the country and in July 1905 it completed a lap at a speed of 73.75mph at the Morris Park racetrack in the Bronx, New York. The success resulted in White sales rising to 1015 cars in 1905 and 1534 the following year, overtaking the production of the Stanley works.

White cars were to have more publicity over the years. One was to have the distinction of being the only car to take part in the inaugural parade for President Theodore Roosevelt, the first President to drive a car himself when he took to the wheel of a White in Puerto Rico in 1906. Up to this time, the car company had simply been a subsidiary of the White Sewing Machine Company, but that year it became a separate organization, with $2.5 million capital and a new factory in New York, employing a thousand men. Unlike the Stanley brothers, however, White were not completely wedded to steam and by 1910, they experimented with a gasoline car. They were impressed with the result and abandoned steam car production the following year.

One company advanced the steam car to a degree of sophistication unmatched by any of its competitors, Doble. The firm had its origins in an even older form of power. Lester Allan Doble invented the Pelton wheel, a form of impulse water turbine that proved highly successful and made him a wealthy man. It was his four sons – Abner, William, John and Warren who decided to develop steam cars. Abner started building his first steam car, with the help of his brothers, while still a sixteen-year old schoolboy. It was based on a wrecked White vehicle but had a redesigned engine. It was not a huge success, and Abner left school to study at MIT. He did not stay long, but decided that he would be better off working with his brothers to develop their steam car ideas. One of their first products, known as Model B, incorporated an efficient condenser that increased the range of the car to such an extent that it could travel for 1500 miles without stopping to take on water. It suffered like all early steam cars from the time it took to get up steam but once under way its performance was far better than the most popular vehicle of the period – the Model T Ford. Whereas the Ford could, with luck, get up to speeds of 50mph, it took nearly three quarters of a minute to get there from a standing start. The Doble could reach 60mph in a very respectable fifteen seconds.

In 1915, Abner drove a Model B to Detroit, which was already home to the Ford factory and was well on its way to being established as the largest centre of car manufacture in the world.

Not unreasonably, he had decided that if he could obtain capital for the Doble car anywhere in America it had to be Detroit. He was successful in raising $200,000, enough to start work on a new model that was to incorporate some radical new thinking. The Model C or Detroit was a remarkable vehicle for its time. One big difference between this and earlier models was that it had an ignition system similar to that in other non-steam cars. There was no longer any need to light pilots and heat up systems; it only required the turn of a key. That was a great selling point, but what happened after initial ignition was also quite different from anything used in earlier steam cars. The car had a new type of flash boiler. The fuel was atomised and ignited with a spark plug, and the temperature raised by an electric fan. This heated the feedwater contained in vertical tubes. This section was separated from the actual steam unit by heat resistant metal. Heat was controlled automatically by means of quartz rods in a tray beneath the boiler. As the tray expanded, it pushed up the rods to close off the burners; then as it cooled, dropped back down to open them again. The controls were simple. If you think back to the complex system of hand and foot controls of the Stanley, one can see just how attractive the Doble must have seemed to potential customers. There was a steering wheel, a foot-operated throttle, another foot pedal for varying the cut-off point and reversing and a third for the brakes. The waiting time between turning the ignition key and being ready to drive off was a modest 90 seconds.

When the Model B was shown at the New York Motor Show it was a huge success, with thousands of orders placed. But in the event, it proved less satisfactory than the test model had suggested and only a few were actually built and sold. Doble set about making improvements, resulting in a new model D, but that too was only built in small quantities and the designers were back at their drawing boards. When it appeared in 1922, the new Model E was far and away the most spectacular steam car built at the time. It had a newly designed 4-cylinder engine, which was in effect two 2-cylinder compound engines set back to back. There was a monotube boiler, in which water was passed up through coils towards the burner. The boiler worked at a pressure of 750psi and the superheated steam reached the cylinders at a temperature of 400°C.

The Model E is a classic road vehicle, with a magnificent performance for its day; it could accelerate from start to 40mph in just eight seconds and had a top speed of over 100mph. It did,

A view beneath the bonnet of a classic E-type Doble steamer. It shows the flash boiler; the actual engine is situated just in front of the rear axle.

however, suffer from one disadvantage; it was very expensive. A top of the range model cost $11.200 – over $150,000 today. Not surprisingly less than fifty were sold and among the wealthy who bought one was Howard Hughes; his Model E still survives.

Technically, the Doble cars were brilliant but they were not a financial success; they were too expensive and too slowly produced. The company was eventually sold to George and William Besler, who continued to experiment with steam power in some unlikely ways, including building and flying a steam-powered aeroplane. Abner Doble and his brother Warren continued to act as consultants on steam power, travelling widely and we shall meet them again in the next chapter, across the Atlantic in Britain. Few steam cars were manufactured after 1930, though many continued in use. Those who had held on to theirs in Britain during the Second World War had an advantage over other car owners. Petrol might be virtually unobtainable, but they could usually find some sort of fuel to keep their machines going. There were some experiments in the late 1940s, mainly by large companies hoping to find a way of avoiding the foul emissions that were causing pollution in crowded streets, but nothing ever went on into mass production.

A new form of transport started to become popular in the second half of the nineteenth century and actually received its first official notice and regulation in the 1878 Highways and Locomotives: the bicycle. By then, engineers had already come up with the idea of substituting steam power for pedal power, but there is some doubt over which machine should receive the accolade as the first steam-powered cycle. Contenders are the Michaux-Perreaux steam velocipede and the Roper steam velocipede. As both were constructed at much the same time between 1867 and 1869, and quite independently, the former in France and the latter in America, it seems reasonable to let them share the honours. Were these the first motorbikes? Again, there is controversy, from those who say a motorbike has to be powered by an internal combustion motor and thus, the first was the one designed by Daimler. The Oxford English Dictionary defines 'motor' as 'an agent or force that produces mechanical motion' and on that definition a steam engine certainly qualifies. But even quibblers have to concede these were the first powered cycles.

The Michaux-Perreaux machine was a joint enterprise. The starting point was the Michaux bicycle. This was a curious device, with a sprung saddle, curved iron frame and the pedals set on the front wheel. It was the first to go into large scale production from a factory, turning out 400 models a year. When it arrived in Britain

This Doble E22 of 1925 looks exactly what it is; a handsome, fast, sporting vehicle. Cars such as this could reach speeds in excess of a hundred miles an hour and could raise steam in less than a minute.

THE GREATEST
MECHANICAL
EXHIBITION
IN THE WORLD.

THE
STEAM
BUGGY!

Pronounced by scientific men to be the most wonderful invention of modern times. It can be driven, with two persons in it, 150 miles a day, upon common roads. It is light and strong, and can be managed better than any horse, and can be driven faster than any person dare to ride. Will match it against any trotting horse in the world.

THE ONLY
Steam Velocipede
IN THE WORLD.

Pronounced a perfect triumph in mechanism. It can be driven up any hill, and will out speed any horse in the world.

TO BE SEEN AT
600 BROADWAY.

ADMISSION ....25 Cents.

A misleading advert for the Roper velocipede; it was not the only one in the world, the Michaux-Perreaux velocipede was already in production in France.

it was nicknamed 'the boneshaker' – having once ridden a similar boneshaker I can testify to the name being entirely appropriate! Louis-Guillaume Parreaux was a French inventor, whose career began at the very early age of just twelve when he designed a gun hidden away inside a walking cane. At the age of 25 he moved from his native Normandy to Paris, where he continued to produce a wide range of inventions, including a new type of lock mechanism, a powered circular saw and a very accurate micrometer screw gauge. He developed a small, single cylinder steam engine that was fuelled by burning alcohol, and it was this engine that he was to fit to the Michaux boneshaker

The Michaux velocipede was adapted by changing the straight upper frame to a curved one to provide space for the engine. The pedals were removed and the drive to the rear wheel was provided by a pair of leather belts. The rider had a pressure gauge mounted in front and a hand controlled regulator for the steam. Rather alarmingly, there were no brakes. Perreaux took out a patent in December 1869 and here at least there is no controversy – this was the first patent for a steam-powered bicycle. He went on to develop his ideas. Only one of the original version of the bicycle was built, but he went on to build a tricycle version that was exhibited in the Industrial Exposition in Paris in 1884. The engine was similar to the original with a working pressure of around 50psi. It was said to be capable of speeds up to 18mph and carried enough water for two to three hours of travel.

Sylvester H. Roper was another precocious engineer, building a stationary steam engine at the age of 12 and a small steam locomotive two years later, even though he had never seen actual examples of either type of engine. In 1854, at the age of twenty-one, he moved to Boston, where his inventive skills appeared in numerous ways, designing a sewing machine and a hot air engine. During the American Civil War, he worked at the Springfield Armory, where he made a number of important improvements to firearm mechanisms. At some time around 1867, he began working on a steam velocipede. As with the French steam bike it was based on a conventional boneshaker. The water tank situated near the front of the crossbar had a shaped top so that it was also the driver's seat. The two-cylinder engine was between the wheels, and was fitted with a sloping chimney that emerged behind the rider. Steam was fed to two cylinders from a boiler angled towards the driver and they were connected to a crank that provided drive for the back wheel. The handlebar was solid with wooden grips that acted as a throttle; unlike the modern motor bike twist grip, the driver turned the whole bar. It was turned forward to open the steam inlet valve and in the opposite direction to close it and apply a brake to the rear wheel. The exhaust steam went up the chimney providing forced draft to the firebox beneath the boiler. It did not go into production, though Roper continued to make improvements.

In 1884 he was approached by Colonel Albert Pope, who wanted a powered pacing machine for his cycle racing team. He owned the Columbia safety bike, and one of these provided the basic frame for the steam pacer. This time Roper used a single cylinder, coal-fired steam engine, generally working at a pressure of 150psi. It was capable of reaching speeds of 40mph. Roper was very proud of his machine and regularly rode one himself, which he claimed could 'climb any hill and outrun any horse'. In 1896 he was invited to demonstrate his pacer at the banked cycle racing track, the Charles River velodrome in Cambridge, Mass. He demonstrated how it could be used to pace the race team and then raced the leading professional cyclist of the day, easily beating him, and was timed as lapping at about 30mph. He then decided to give a demonstration at full power, reaching speeds of over 40mph. Then the spectators saw the machine first wobble then fall over and when they reached the inventor, he was dead. He had died of a heart attack at the age of 73.

The age of the steam car and the steam bike was comparatively short lived and had comparatively small impact on the development of road transport in general. But when we look at road haulage and the new developments of the late nineteenth and early twentieth centuries, then there is a very different story to tell of commercial success.

Chapter Ten

The Steam Waggon

One of the earliest references to a steam wagon can be found in the *Huddersfield Chronicle* in May 1860. A local boiler manufacturer, William Arnold, had designed a 'Steam Horse' to transport his boilers around the country. The technical description is rather limited; it had a conventional locomotive type boiler and engine mounted on a wrought iron frame. The vehicle was 32 ft long and around 8ft wide, mounted on four wheels and said to be capable of carrying loads of 60 tons. But as Arnold only ever intended the machine for his own use he seems to have had no interest in developing it any further. There were a few other spasmodic attempts to develop steam wagons along similar lines, but thanks to the restrictions imposed by the Red Flag Act, there was very little incentive to develop any new form of road transport. The slow, lumbering but powerful traction engine was able to cope with the traffic and if it could not go very fast that was of little importance when it had to follow a man trudging along in front with his flag. A number of engineers saw a possible solution to the problems of road traffic in the form of a road locomotive, pulling a train of carriages or trucks. At the end of the nineteenth century, the main rail network was considered more or less complete. But it still left many, largely rural, areas without any nearby rail access. The answer was thought to lie with cheap versions of the main line, run with light rails and slow trains. The Light Railways Act of 1896 empowered companies to build and run such lines without the huge expense of getting an Act of Parliament; they only had to apply for a Light Railways Order. It was an undoubted success and hundreds of miles of track were added to the system. But the road engineers thought this might be unnecessary. They felt that with road locomotives you could do the same job without laying any track at all. There was a general feeling among many who advocated this form of road transport that their biggest opponents were the powerful railway interests who disliked the notion of any form of rival appearing. The schemes came to nothing, largely because of the same laws restricting speeds that hampered all forms of advance for steam vehicles.

Two views of a Thorneycroft steam wagon with the bodywork removed, showing on the left the vertical boiler and chimney passing through the cab, and on the right, the engine beneath the main frame.

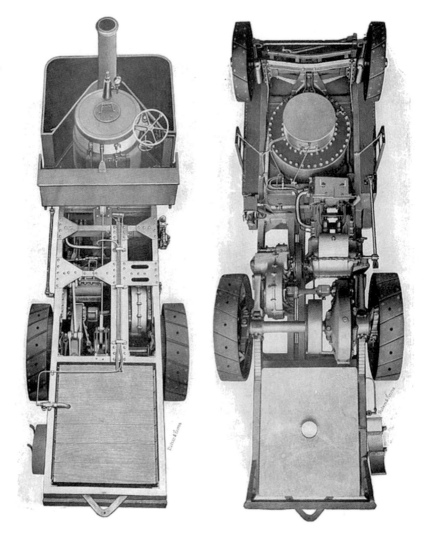

The situation changed with the passing of the Locomotive on Highways Act of 1896 that set a new speed limit of 12 miles an hour. The development of the motor car brought a powerful lobby arguing for even higher limits – and in some cases for no limits at all. The Motor Car Act of 1903 set the limit at 20mph. There was now a real incentive to develop lighter, faster machines – particularly with the threat of competition from the new diesel and petrol engine powered vehicles. One response to the new situation came from the rather cumbersomely named Liverpool Self Propelled Traffic Association. They set up trials in 1898, 1899 and 1901 to find vehicles that could take advantage of the improved speed limits. One of the first entrants was a van with an oil-fired

engine that came from a rather surprising source, the engineering firm of Thorneycroft.

John Isaac Thorneycroft came from an unlikely background for a man who would become a highly successful engineer. Both his parents were sculptors – his father's best known work is the statue of Boadicea on the Embankment in London. The son showed more practical than artistic skills, so his father taught him metal working at their riverside home in Chiswick. In 1862, at the age of nineteen, he built himself a steam launch, which was so successful that he was able to persuade his father, who owned land by the river, to set up John with his own factory. Thorneycroft moved on from his successful steam launches – one of his vessels was the first that was able to follow the annual Oxford-Cambridge boat race and keep pace with the rowers – to building fast steam torpedo boats. The company relocated to a larger shipyard in Southampton, where they were able to build even bigger ships, concentrating on fast attack vessels such as destroyers. In 1896 they built their first experimental steam wagon. It was a curious affair that owed quite

The Foden family; William Foden, son of the founder, second from left with his three sons and grandson pose in front of the appropriately named 'Pride of Edwin' a 5-ton wagon built in 1916 and supplied new to the Portsmouth and Gosport Gas Works.

A Foden wagon supplied to the War Ministry with its two man crew, seen here on the Western Front during the First World War.

a lot to its predecessors in river launches – and it was a launch engine that provided the power, fed by a water tube boiler. The drive was transmitted to the front wheels but the steering to the rear. The following year they sold their first wagon, a dustcart that was bought by Chiswick Council. The machine that they brought along to the Liverpool trial was Thorneycroft No.1 They began building steam wagons and received an order from the army to provide wagons for South Africa, where the Boer War was being fought. Kitchener himself noted that though the petrol lorries 'did very well, Thorneycroft's are the best'. The company went on to improve their designs. They built an articulated six-wheeler and their other wagons with rigid frames were fitted with Weston multi-disc clutches. This enabled them to change gear on the move, something most traction engines of the time were unable to do – they had to be brought to a halt first. They introduced self-feeding furnaces to provide steam for high-speed engines. They were powerful machines; the three-ton wagon could carry a four ton load on the back and could pull another three ton on a trailer. In spite of their success, however, the company's interest in steam wagons proved to be short lived. They built their first petrol-engined truck in 1902 and by 1907 they had abandoned steam on the road.

The first Liverpool trial attracted surprisingly few entries. It was hoped that the new developments with internal combustion vehicles would produce some interesting results but none of them was able to move the comparatively modest load of two tons round the set course. By the time of the third trial, there were three steam wagons to share the first prize, Leyland, Thorneycroft and Coulthard, with a special silver medal for Mann's. The last were to be among the most important pioneers of the new form of transport.

James Mann had originally trained as an engineer at the works of J & H McLaren of Leeds who had an established business manufacturing a variety of traction engines. He was later to gain more experience with the famous Marshalls of Gainsborough. Another McLaren trainee was Sidney Charlesworth who also gained more experience, this time with Garretts of Leiston. In 1894 they got together to form Mann & Charlesworth in Hunslet, not far from the McLaren works, producing parts for steam engines. Their major contribution was the single-eccentric reversing gear, which greatly simplified the whole reversing process and gave smoother control for changes to the cut-off point, where steam was simply allowed to expand in the cylinder. Then in 1898 they received a request from Philip Parmiter of Tisbury in Wiltshire for a steam farm cart. They used the front end of a normal traction engine and attached a roller at the back to carry the cart platform. This was the forerunner of what became known as 'overtype' steam wagons that look, as this one did, like a combination of traction engine and conventional truck. The cab and vertical boiler are situated behind the chimney and firebox. The alternative, the 'undertype' wagon has the engine below the chassis, with the cab right at the front of the vehicle.

Charlesworth left the company in 1898 and the following year a new company, Mann's Patent Steam Car and Wagon Company, was formed. Mann was now able to build on his initial success and began developing a whole series of steam wagons, mainly either 3-ton or 5-ton versions. He was so successful that in 1901 he was able to move to larger premises in Pepper Road, Hunslet fitted out with all the latest machine tools. The wagons were adapted for all kinds of uses from brewers' drays to gully cleaning wagons and the company had many years of success, producing other steam vehicles including patching rollers for road repairs and tractors. Their most advanced model appeared in 1924, the Mann Express wagon, featuring a totally enclosed cab, high-speed engine and shaft drive. The design was impeccable but it was not a financial success and by 1929 the works had closed down. The company was bought by Atkinson Walker Wagons Ltd. but the following year it was sold again, this time to Scammell, who were later to become famous for their high-powered diesel trucks.

James Mann was not the only member of the family to get involved in steam wagon construction in the early days. His brother George took out a patent for a new type of wagon with Joseph Clayton, director of Clayton, Son & Co., also based in Hunslet. Their first wagons were produced from their small works in Leeds in 1901 under the name of the 'Yorkshire Steam Motor Company' The following year they were bought by Deighton's Patent Flue and Tube Company and established as a subsidiary under the name 'Yorkshire Patent Steam Wagon Company'. There were to be more changes over the years, including a spell when they toyed with manufacturing motor cars as the Yorkshire Commercial Motor Company. That was a short-lived experiment and they reverted back to the older name.

The first vehicles to be produced were powered by a two-cylinder compound engine, with the high-pressure cylinder at one side of the chassis and the low pressure on the other. The valves were worked by means of a single-eccentric reversing gear very similar to the Mann; it is possible that the brothers co-operated on this. There were sliding gears on the crankshaft offering two speed variations and the rear wheels were driven through gearing. They brought out a new model in 1906 with a very different arrangement. The engine was enclosed in a cast-iron case and mounted vertically inside the cab. The engine now had Hancock valve gears and the drive was by chain to the rear axle, with a three-speed gearbox. The boilers were mainly supplied by the neighbouring firm of Clayton. The new engine was so successful that when it was entered for the Royal Automobile Club Trials it was awarded a gold medal in its class. There were a few improvements over the next three years, but by 1909 the design work was over and there were no more changes until 1931.

The Yorkshire did have a brief life under a new guise in 1918 when, instead of the normal truck arrangement, an omnibus body was added behind the cab. Like the wagon it had three speeds – 5, 8 and 16mph – and was sent for service in Grimsby. It did not have a successful career. Just one year after it went into service it was in a collision with a tramcar and was converted back into a wagon. The old bus superstructure went onto a petrol engine chassis. The experiment was not repeated.

Among the few who responded quickly to the opening for a new generation of steam wagons was Brazil, Straker – later Straker Squire. Formed in Bristol in 1893 they began by building engines for steam wagons. They developed their own version of the De Dion boiler. It was a vertical water-tube type consisting of four concentric tubes, the inner and outer pairs joined to create a double water jacket, the space in between being filled with a number of straight water tubes. The central section was higher than the outer, creating the same effect as a steam dome on a railway locomotive. This arrangement also allowed room for water levels to move safely within the boiler when the vehicle was on a steep hill. It was fired by dropping the fuel down a central chute.

In 1901 they decided that they would build their own complete wagon with a single chain drive to the rear axle. It was fitted with large wheels, very similar to those of a traction engine of the time, that had to be set outside the main frame. By the following year, they had changed the pattern by adopting smaller wheels, giving the vehicle a much more conventional appearance. By 1905 they had changed again, this time building an overtype wagon with a locomotive boiler.

One potential customer for steam wagons was the War Department. They had already had some success with steam wagons in the Boer War, but now they wanted to make sure they got the best possible. Although Kitchener, as mentioned earlier, was pleased with his wagons, the army top brass in general were notoriously opposed to almost any form of mechanised transport; many still saw warfare in terms of charging cavalry with drawn swords. Famously when Winston Churchill authorised the development of what were

Two more
Foden wagons photographed on service during the First World War. They are being used to transport sanitation boilers that were needed to get rid of the lice infestations that plagued the men in the trenches.

Inside the cab of a Foden, looking much closer to the footplate of a steam locomotive than the cab of a road vehicle.

then called landships, armoured vehicles that could move over any terrain, he kept the army head Kitchener in the dark, fearing the top brass would veto the experiments. The new machines were misleadingly referred to as being water carriers for use in Mesopotamia; at the works this title generally got shortened first to 'water tanks' then simply 'tanks' – a name that has remained in use ever since. The first tanks were built by the well known traction engine manufacturer, Foster. But the story of developing powered vehicles for the army goes back a little further to trials held at Aldershot in 1901. Straker's was among the companies taking part but the winner wasThorneycroft, which was said to be the best over rough ground. Perhaps their role in the Boer War had helped move the decision their way, but most expert observers felt they had made the wrong choice; they felt that the best vehicle was the Foden entry.

Edwin Foden was born in 1841 and when he was fifteen years old he was apprenticed first to the agricultural machinery manufacturers Plant & Hancock and then at the famous railway works in Crewe. At nineteen he returned to Plant & Hancock and had obviously learned his profession well for he was soon offered a partnership. When George Hancock retired, Foden took over the running of the company which was then renamed Edwin Foden & Sons. Under Foden, they began producing a variety of industrial engines and in 1882 they produced their first traction engine. The prototype proved a success and they went into full production. By 1887 they were producing compound engines for their vehicles, with much improved efficiency. Like many other companies, they saw the relaxation of regulations as an opportunity to develop a new type of steam wagon. Their three-ton wagon was the one that took part in the War Office trials and it was faster and more economical than the Thorneycroft. It was a disappointment not to win but when Thorneycroft abandoned steam for diesel, the company was able to send their wagons over to France during the First World War, where they proved very effective. Nevertheless, they played a comparatively minor role compared with the use of horses. It has been estimated that over a million horses were used on the battlefield and suffered great losses.

A Foden C Type of 1928 in the livery of the London brewer Fuller, Smith & Turner, now simply known as Fuller's. Many wagon manufacturers offered wagons specially adapted for brewers.

The company settled in premises at Sandbach, Cheshire, where they produced a wide range of vehicles, mostly overtype. By the 1930s, however, they produced a very successful range of

The high and low pressure cylinders of a Foden compound engine, with the gear box and boiler feed pump.

undertype wagons, the Speed-6 and Speed-12. They had pneumatic tyres, enclosed cabs and electric lights and were capable of speeds of 50mph. The Speed-6 was 4-wheeled, the 12 was 6-wheeled. When the founder's son, Edwin Richard Foden, took over the business he decided to abandon steam in favour of diesel. Foden continued to prosper, but their days of steam had come to an end.

Many traditional manufacturers turned to wagon manufacturing in the early twentieth century, including Fowler of Leeds. They had already shown themselves to be prepared to try the unorthodox. As early as 1868 they were experimenting with undertype traction engines, with the cylinders and gearing beneath the boiler and in 1881 they were the first to introduce compound cylinders to traction engines. By the early twentieth century, a lot of their efforts went into ploughing engines and one of their biggest customers was Russia. This proved unfortunate when revolution engulfed that country and Fowler's were left with a large number of engines, ordered but never paid for.

Like many other companies, they considered building wagons for use in the First World War and produced a prototype in 1915, but the factory was far too busy producing munitions and various types of traction engine – doubly so when the government put in

an order for 90 pairs of ploughing engines in 1917. The prototype went into use at the works and was only eventually taken out of service in 1932. The first new steam wagon only went into production in 1927. But soon the company was producing a wide range of vehicles. One of their first successes was with a gutter cleaner. Many road surfaces were still far from perfect and all sorts of gunge got washed down into the drains, causing blockages and flooding. The cleaner had a vacuum tank on top of the body that could be evacuated by means of a steam injector in half a second. A flexible hose was then dropped down into the drain to suck up the loose material – in other words it acted like a giant vacuum cleaner. The waste material was drawn into the main sludge tank, which had a sloping floor. Once the tank was full, the vehicle went off to wherever the waste was to be dumped, and once the door of the tank was opened the sludge simply slid out. The machine could also be adapted for water spraying to keep streets clean, so it could be kept constantly in use in one form or the other.

Fowler also offered more conventional wagons with a variety of bodies, including double-decker versions and furniture vans. Their catalogue is interesting in giving an insight into drivers' working environment, 'For better protection of the driver in bad weather we

Many companies that had begun by manufacturing traction engines turned to building steam wagons in the twentieth century. This tipping truck was built by Garrett and has an unusual cab, with the driver's section slightly protruding to give a clearer view.

A fine example of a Super Sentinel, one of the most successful steam wagons ever built, seen at a rally.

can fit, when required, special wind screens and side curtains on all sides of the cab, giving very complete protection'. Few modern truck drivers would consider 'side curtains' to be 'complete protection'. Other special offers were made for what would now be considered essentials:

> 'For wagons which have a considerable amount of night work to do, we can supply either electric lighting equipment, or acetylene headlights.'

All the Fowler wagons featured their own patented vertical boiler that contained a large number of curved fire tubes, in which they claimed eddies in the hot gases were more effective in transferring heat to the water than straight tubes. The compound engine had the two cylinders arranged in a 'V' working on a single throw crank and working at a pressure of 225psi. They were very proud of the performance of their engines and in the catalogue described a test carried out in Natal when a wagon carried a 6½ ton load up a two mile hill, with gradients varying from 1 in 10 to 1 in 7. It made the trip 'at good speed' and at the end of the run the boiler pressure had only dropped by 5 pounds.

One company, however, stood out from all others as manufacturers of steam wagons – except that they did not follow the normal spelling and called their vehicles 'waggons' to distinguish them from lesser breeds. That company was Sentinel. Their story begins in 1875 when Stephen Alley and John Alexander MacLellan began manufacturing valves at the Sentinel works in Glasgow. In 1903 they took over the Simpson & Bibby company, who owned an ironworks at Horsehay in Shropshire. Perhaps the initial attraction had been to secure a regular supply of high quality iron but the company had also taken out a number of patents for steam vehicles. Alley & MacLellan decided to follow up on this and invited the two previous owners, together with their designer, Daniel Simpson, to join them at their works in Scotland in 1903. Two years later, the first Sentinel waggon appeared, known as the 'Standard'. By 1914, the business was so successful that they decided they needed new premises and chose a site in Shrewsbury. In a remarkable modern approach, they prefabricated the new factory in Glasgow and then took it down to Shropshire to be erected. As they also needed a new workforce, they built a model village for the men and their families and also supplied hot water from the factory for both normal washing use and for central heating.

The next four years were largely taken up with orders for the army, providing some 200 vehicles over the four year period. At the end of the war, Stephen Alley sold his shares in Alley & MacLellan and set up a new company, Sentinel Waggon Works and there was to be a major reorganisation in 1920. Up to this time virtually all steam vehicles had been built by bringing the parts to the site where the vehicle would be assembled; Sentinel now adopted the assembly line approach, pioneered by Henry Ford.

Over the next few years, Sentinel introduced a variety of different models. The standard was phased out in the 1920s but by the time production came to an end, 3,750 had been built, more than any other make of steam road vehicle, before or since. Improvements were made on the basic design resulting in the Super model that appeared in 1923 and the first double-geared waggon, the first of the DG class, was introduced in 1927. In 1931 a new consultant arrived in Shrewsbury from America, Abner Doble, who was to stay with the company for the next four years. In that time a number of changes were introduced. The Sentinel-Doble lorry had a two-cylinder compound engine on the back axle, and automatic stoking was introduced. The latter was an important development. One of the problems that steam wagons faced in competition with

Sentinel did
a deal with the
Skoda company
of Czechoslovakia,
allowing them to
build their wagons
under licence. This
is the Czech version
of the Super.

their diesel rivals was the need for a two-man crew. Now only a driver would be needed. Sentinel were a remarkably progressive firm and by 1933 they had produced one of the most successful steam wagons ever built, the Sentinel S. The company also made an agreement with Skoda of Plzen, in what was then Czechoslovakia, for the Czech company to import Super Sentinels and later to manufacture them under licence.

Sentinel continued in business for an extraordinarily long time, although their output was not limited to steam wagons and they developed a very successful line of railway locomotives. Nevertheless, they continued manufacturing their waggons until after the end of the Second World War and received an order for a hundred S6 waggons from the Argentine Government in 1950. The following year, the last steam Sentinel left the Shrewsbury works.

Britain was not the only country manufacturing steam wagons. The Doble brothers travelled the globe advising various companies on steam vehicles. Before he went to Sentinel, Abner visited New Zealand where he helped to develop steam buses for the Auckland

Transport Board. Between 1932 and 1933 Warren advised the Henschel Company of Kassel in Germany, who went on to build a variety of steam trucks, including delivery vehicles for the German railway system, the Deutsche Bahn. They were very efficient wagons, working at high pressure with flash boilers. One German manufacturer looked to Britain for inspiration. Schwartzkopff of Berlin built Thorneycroft based vehicles under licence, while Hannoveresche Maschinenbau Aktien Gessellschaft, a name not surprisingly later reduced to the more manageable HANOMAG, developed wagons based on Stoltz high-pressure boilers. Various other companies, usually based on locomotive works, built steam trucks in various European countries but none was of very significant size.

In America, there were many small producers of steam wagons and some of the larger firms such as Buffalo also produced a few vehicles. One surprising innovation was a vehicle produced in America in 1904 that used a steam turbine to generate electricity for a motor that provided the actual power to drive the wheels. The field was, however, dominated by Britain. Of the known 160 known manufacturers, ninety-two were based in Britain. Production had a brief spurt in Europe immediately after the Second World War, mainly because of the desperate shortage of oil and petrol. But it soon petered out and production ended.

CHAPTER ELEVEN

The End of the Road

The development of the internal combustion engine posed an immediate threat to the dominance of steam power. Among the first to succumb to competition were the agricultural traction engines, especially ploughing sets. Where heavy traction engines had to be kept clear of the area to be ploughed because of the damage they would cause, the new diesel tractors presented no such problem. American companies led the way in developing the farm tractor. The International Harvest Company was formed in 1902 from a group of agricultural machinery manufacturers, including McCormick who had already developed the mechanical reaper. The other, almost inevitably, was that pioneer of cheap mechanical transport, Henry Ford. He started building lightweight Fordson tractors in 1916. The idea caught on rapidly in America where oil was cheap but attracted little interest in Britain, where coal remained by far the cheaper fuel. The outbreak of war in 1914 was to change everything.

The German submarine campaign was having a devastating effect on British shipping and particularly on food supplies. In the earlier nineteenth century, Britain's cereal industry had been protected by the Corn Laws, but when they were repealed the way was open to import grain from America and Canada. Many British farmers found it more profitable to turn their fields over to pasture. The arrival of the railways had made it easier to bring fresh milk and produce to customers; as a result, 75 per cent of Britain's wheat was being imported by the beginning of the twentieth century. Now that supply was threatened and the government realised that drastic action was needed. Manpower was short on the land, as so many young men were now in the army, so an obvious answer was to invest in mechanisation.

The first British tractor to be powered by an oil engine had been built by Richard Hornsby in 1896. He took a great deal of care over development, trying out designs on his own farm before going into production. He later developed a 'chain-track' version powered by a paraffin engine and saw his tractors as having a military use as well as being valuable for agriculture – the chain track vehicle

was seen as a prototype tank, though the army were not interested. This motor tractor proved to be no more attractive to farmers in the pre-war years than its other use as a tank was to the army. Consequently, few vehicles were produced, so when the need for mechanisation became urgent the government had no option; they began importing tractors from America.

There was a modest start, when the government set up ploughing units, each equipped with eleven tractors and trained staff to do work under contract. It was not a huge success, largely because the ploughs provided by the individual farmers were not always up to the job. The alternative scheme allowed farmers to lease tractors on very easy terms with an option to buy them at the end of the war. It has been estimated that over the war years some 3,000 machines were brought over from America. The most common import was the Titan, built by the International Harvest Company of Chicago, a cumbersome beast of a machine with a top speed of 3mph.

By the end of the war, there were now a great many tractors at work, and improvements soon followed. Henry Ford set up a new company to build tractors in America in 1918 and agreed to start production in Britain as well. One major improvement was made by a British engineer, Henry Ferguson. He was an enterprising young man – he built and flew his own aeroplane at the age of 25.

The development of tractors such as this photographed with a reaper early in the twentieth century helped to make the agricultural traction engine obsolete.

He developed a rigid combination of plough and tractor and was eventually to go into partnership with Ford, building tractors at Dagenham. All this amounted to serious competition to the steam ploughing teams. Now a farmer could plough his own fields and the job could be passed to just one farm worker, instead of the three-man crew needed for the steam plough. It was to prove fatal and ploughing traction engines soon ceased production altogether.

It was not only the ploughing engine that was threatened by changes down on the farm. Throughout most of agricultural history, the cutting and threshing of grain had been two quite distinct operations. However, by the second half of the nineteenth century, attempts were being made to combine the operations. One of the first combine harvesters able to cut wide swathes of grain was introduced in America in 1860, but it needed a team of up to thirty horses. It was a practical machine for the vast expanses of the wheat growing prairie states but of little value in the small fields of Europe. By 1895, a power source had been added to work the machinery and

The famous Model T Ford; the mass-produced car was the greatest threat to the steam car, not least because it was far cheaper to buy.

by 1911, the Holt Company of Stockton, California had installed an internal combustion engine to do the job. The advantages of having the combined operations was obvious and threatened the old system of threshing using a portable or traction engine; but a far greater threat appeared in the 1930s when the Massey-Harris Company in the States produced the first self-propelled combine harvester. Like the steam plough, the agricultural traction engine's days were numbered.

Road traction was not immediately affected to the same extent as the agricultural engines, largely because the first petrol and diesel trucks were not very efficient. This was highlighted when the British engineer Harry Lawson inaugurated the Emancipation Run from London to Brighton in 1896 to celebrate the relaxation of the laws on road transport. Recognising that many of the early vehicles were likely to have problems along the way, he arranged for a Daimler lorry to carry spares of all kinds. Unfortunately, it was the Daimler itself that proved most in need of assistance, breaking down several times en route! Even as the design improved, the traction engine and steam wagon manufacturers felt confident of keeping the opposition at bay. Competition increased at the end of the First World War, when huge numbers of army surplus trucks appeared on the market at knock-down process, but the steam men still proclaimed the superiority of their vehicles. Fowler listed the advantages of using their steam tractors:

1. Low cost of haulage, using cheap fuel, with low maintenance costs, long working life, and great reliability.
2. No time wasted loading or unloading. Extra trailers or wagons can be used at loading and unloading points, so that the engine is always busily employed on hauling. This makes a vital difference in many cases in the quantity of goods hauled and cost per ton.
3. Able to travel over rough or unmade ground with the help of its large driving wheels.
4. Able to extricate itself by means of its winding rope when in difficulties.
5. Available for all kinds of hoisting and hauling work with the winding rope.
6. Unequalled for rough work in partially developed countries.
7. Always available for stationary belt driving work as an alternative to hauling.

The Fowler company was at least prepared to admit that in some circumstances, the lorry that was so much faster than the steam tractor might be preferable, but they were very keen to stress the advantages of the latter in the colonies where roads were likely to be less than perfect. The lorry was liable to get bogged down, where the tractor – even if it did get stuck – could haul itself out again with the winch. Then the company was able to look at the differences between the internal combustion truck and the steam wagon. Their first point was that fuel costs for a steam wagon were roughly half those for a petrol wagon; Britain still had huge reserves of coal being worked but had to import oil. They admitted that at first, the steam wagon was far slower than the rival but claimed that this was no longer the case. There was also a case to be made that the steam wagon was likely to last far longer, and they quoted Inland Revenue figures, which allowed 20 per cent depreciation to be written off for a petrol wagon, but only 15 per cent for steam. This, they said, was only to be expected 'as a result of the smoother drive, ample reserve of power and absence of vibration'. The final argument was that the steam wagon had the advantage of not possessing various parts that 'were most likely to cause trouble on the road' – the magneto, carburettor and clutch.

The steam wagon arguments look quite convincing but what was perhaps not appreciated at the time was the speed with which the petrol and diesel trucks would be developed. As time went on, the initial costs came down due to the large scale of production and those 'troublesome' parts ceased to cause any problems. Nevertheless in the 'thirties, it seemed the steam wagon was holding its place in the market, largely because of its well established dependability. What Fowler had not foreseen was new government legislation that increased the tax on heavier vehicles. The lorries had the advantage that they generally ran on pneumatic tyres instead of the solid rubber tyres of the steam wagon and they only needed to have one fuel tank, where the steamer had to carry both its fuel and a large supply of water. The result was a rapid move away from steam; it was estimated that in the early 1930s, some five thousand steam wagons were taken out of service. The inevitable effect was that manufacturers also either turned to the internal combustion engine or went out of business.

Steam wagons continued in use in small numbers during the Second World War and several were brought out of retirement at the time of the Suez Crisis of 1956, when Britain suddenly found

The end of an era; a portable engine rusting away at a stone quarry on Portland.

the petrol pumps running dry. But manufacture had ceased long before that. The same competition faced by steam wagons was also faced by the steam car and was, if anything, even more intense. The motor car developed very rapidly, and, thanks to Henry Ford's improved production methods, the price of a modest car fell steeply. The Model T was introduced to the world in 1908 with a price tag of $850. Its popularity was immense and by 1927, Ford had turned out around 15 million vehicles and a basic car could be

The end of the commercial use of steam on the roads did not spell the end for steam traction. In August 1953 four traction engine owners got together at Pickering to race each other in a traction engine Derby. The race attracted a good crowd and led to the formation of the Great Yorkshire Traction Engine Club.

bought for as little as $260. The Stanley 740D was admittedly far less basic than the Ford car, popularly known as the 'Tin Lizzie', but even so its price of $3950 meant that only the wealthy could afford to purchase it. And by that date even the most prestigious motor was still cheaper than the Stanley; a new top of the range Cadillac could be bought for just under $3,000. Whatever its merits, the steam car was unable to compete. As with the steam wagon, there was a revival of interest in the steam car during the Second World War, and attempts were made afterwards to develop new models.

The State of California was concerned about pollution, which, given later developments, they were quite right to be, and made various efforts to develop clean steam vehicles. They developed a steam bus, which went into limited service and adapted a 1973 Chevrolet Coupé by adding a steam turbine and fitted a Ford Pinto with a four-cylinder compound steam engine. None of these models appear to ever have gone into production. Several motor companies toyed with the idea of turning to steam but nothing ever came of them. The truth is that the steam engine is intrinsically less efficient than the internal combustion engine, and environmental issues did not arouse the same levels of concern half a century ago that they do – or at any rate should do – today. The steam car was consigned to history.

Logically, that should have been the end of the story of steam on the road. However, many owners had a real affection for their old machines, while others who had admired them in their working days were anxious to see them preserved. By the 1950s, people were looking to see what they could do with old traction engines that were no longer needed for work. The obvious answer was to use them for pleasure. Clubs began to form around the country in which owners could show off their engines – and it soon became apparent that there were a lot of other people interested to see the old beasts in steam even if they did not own one themselves nor were ever likely to do so. The end result was the round of steam rallies that are now a fixture in countries around the world. Rather than go through and try and list every organisation that ever got going, we are going to look at just one that began in Yorkshire in 1953.

The story begins with a race not a rally. On 15 August 1953 four engines lined up outside the Black Swan Inn in Pickering, then made their way to a field in Millers Lane for a traction engine Derby. They raced each other for three laps round the field and the event was won by a Clayton & Shuttleworth engine *Old Glory* with Marshall engine *Surprise* in second place and another Marshall engine *Mary* in third. The event was a success and two more traction engine Derbys were run, attracting more and more engines. The idea of racing traction engines attracted the attention of British film makers and in 1962, such a race formed the basis for the movie *The Iron Maiden*. The *Maiden* of the title was, in fact, a Fowler of 1920 that had begun its working life moving stone from quarries on Portland.

By the time of the 1955 event 18 engines turned up and new contests were introduced including an engine tug-of-war. As well as the traction engines, various vintage and veteran cars and motorcycles put in an appearance. The Derby was well on its way to becoming a fully fledged rally, though that was not to happen until 1962. The success of the rallies led directly to the formation of the Great Yorkshire Traction Engine Club, that continues to organise events right up to the present day, as do many other local clubs and societies.

Traction engines on parade are a popular feature of all modern steam fairs.

Today rallies have become major events in many countries of the world, but few if any are as grand and comprehensive as the annual Great Dorset Steam Fair, begun in 1969. Engines of every conceivable type are on show, not merely going round the parade ring but in many cases being put through their paces, doing the work they built to do. So, ploughing engines do plough the ground, agricultural engines work all kinds of machinery from sawmills to binding machines and haulage engines show what they are made of by hauling spectacularly large loads. And, of course, there is the fairground where showmen's engines provide the power. It now attracts something like 200,000 people every year. Events such as this are big business but ultimately, they depend on the efforts of all those individuals who spend their own money and a great deal of time keeping their precious engines in working order.

I recently visited David Hurley and his family at their home in Lincolnshire, owners of the steam roller that appears on p.83. David became an instant enthusiast when he went to his first steam fair with his parents when he was eight years old and managed to scrounge a ride on an engine. He and his wife Jo crewed other people's engines for a time before buying their own. Acquiring the engine is just the start of the story. Visitors see the engine at rallies looking immaculate and steaming merrily along. But as David said, 'What they don't see is me lying on my back under the engine with ash from the ashcan falling on my face'. Nor are they around to see Jo get up at 6.30 in the morning to light the boiler and stay there to tend it as steam is gently raised. And they are not stopping there; a dilapidated portable engine is sitting in their front garden, waiting to be brought back to life. Both David and Jo are equally enthusiastic, and they have passed on their enthusiasm to their son, Will, and daughter, Becky, who are both enthusiastically ready to keep up the family tradition. They are not exceptional; there are families all around this country and abroad equally willing to put in the cash and hard work that is needed for conservation. And as long as there are people like them who share their ideals, then steam on the road is by no means dead and forgotten.

Locomotive Acts

As the legislation passed by the British Parliament had such an important role to play in the development of steam on the road, readers might find it useful to see the outlines of the main measures that were included in the principal Locomotive Acts.

1861

This Act was actually of some benefit to the users of traction engines, as it prevented the Turnpike Trusts from exhorting huge fees for engines using their roads, by setting out a legal formula. The fees were set per two tons of vehicle weight and equal to the respective tolls for horse-drawn vehicles. Other requirements were that each vehicle must 'consume its own smoke', an early requirement for railway locomotives, which effectively restricted them to using coke as a fuel. There was a minimum width for wheels depending on weight to prevent damaging the road surface. Each locomotive had to have at least two people on board, which would have been normal practice anyway, but a third man was needed if a vehicle was being towed. The owner's name and the vehicle's weight had to be clearly displayed and the engine had to have lights if used at night. The maximum speeds allowed were 10mph in open country and 5mph in built up areas. There was also special provision made for compensating turnpike trustees for any damage caused by the engines.

1865

This was the notorious 'Red Flag Act'. The clauses that gave it the nickname read:

'Firstly, at least three persons shall be employed to drive or conduct such locomotive, and if more than two wagons or carriages be attached to it, an additional person shall be employed, who shall take charge of such wagons or carriages:

'Secondly, one of such persons, while any locomotive is in motion shall precede such locomotive on foot by not less than sixty yards, and shall carry a red flag constantly displayed, and shall warn the riders and drivers of horses of the approach of such locomotives, and shall signal the driver thereof when it shall be necessary to stop, and shall assist horses, and carriages drawn by horses, passing the same,'

The Act contained numerous other regulations. Speeds were limited to 4 miles per hour on the open road and a miserable 2 miles an hour in built up areas. The only member of the crew who would have welcomed the arrival in town was the flag man as his brisk walk was reduced to a slow amble. Penalties for speeding were harsh, with a £10 fine, over £1000 in today's money. Other regulations decreed that the engine could not blow off steam nor use its whistle – which in effect made the whistle entirely useless. Vehicle size was restricted to a weight of 14 tons and a width of 9 feet.

1878

This Act amended the 1865 Act but was chiefly concerned with regulating the ownership and use of roads but it proved valuable to steam vehicle owners, who had often suffered by having to pay prohibitively high tolls set by some Turnpike Trusts. Now the Trusts were being abolished, and charges were standardised depending on the weight of the vehicle and bore a reasonable relationship to charges made on horse-drawn vehicles. Turnpike roads were now to be handed over to local authorities and maintenance costs paid out of the county rates. Routes connecting towns to each other or to railway stations were designated as main roads – the now familiar A and B roads had not yet been introduced. There was one clause that might have worried steam operators. Heavy vehicles that were considered likely to cause excessive wear and tear had to pay towards road maintenance. On the other hand, the regulation that they should consume their own smoke was repealed, so engines could now be fired using coal instead of coke.

1896

This was the Act that opened the way to the development of road transport, whether by steam vehicles or motor cars. It introduced a new class the 'light locomotive', defined as weighing under 3 tons unladen. These no longer needed a third crew member nor his flag, and were permitted to run at up to 14 miles per hour, though local authorities were permitted to reduce this to 12 miles per hour. The passing of the Act was the occasion for a huge celebration by the new motoring community who organised the 'Emancipation Run' from London to Brighton, starting the tradition that survives to the present day.

1898

There was a need to tidy up regulations governing the use of steam vehicles, and the Act contained a number of minor regulations. Among the most important was the requirement of steam traction engines, except agricultural engines, to be licensed by the county council.

Select Bibliography

BIRD, Anthony, *Roads and Vehicles,* Prentice Hall Press, 1969.

BIRD, Anthony, *The Steam Car,* Littlehampton Books, 1975.

BURTON, Anthony, *Richard Trevithick*, Aurum Press, 2000.

EVANS, Richard J., *Steam Cars*, Shire Publications, 1985.

FLETCHER, William, *English and American Steam Carriages*, 1904.

FLETCHER, William, *The History and Development of Steam Locomotives on Common Roads*, 1891.

HANCOCK, Walter, *Narrative of Twelve Years Experiments of Employing Steam- Carriages*, 1838.

HUGHES, W.J. (ed), *Fowler Steam Road Vehicles*, David & Charles, 1976.

HUGHES, W.J. and **THOMAS,** Joseph L., *The Sentinel, Vol 1.*, 1968.

FRANCIS, James, *Walter Hancock*, 1975.

KELLY, Maurice A., *The Overtype Steam Wagon,* Goose and Son, 1971.

KELLY, Maurice A., *The Undertype Steam Wagon*, Goose and Son, 1975.

KENNETT, Pat, *The Foden Story*, Patrick Stephens Ltd, 1978.

MOORE, H.C., *Omnibuses and Cabs*, (reissed Palata Press) 1902.

NORRIS, William, *Modern Steam Road Wagons*, 1906

RAYNOR, Derek, *Steam Wagons*, Shire Publications, 2003.

WHITEHEAD, R.A., *Garratt Wagons, Parts 1 and 2*, R.A. Whitehead and Partners, 1974 and 1975.

WOODBURY, George, *The Story of the Stanley Steamer*, Floyd Clymer, 1967.

Steam on Road Credits

Index